FLORIDA

A Camping Guide

Blair Howard

HUNTER
PUBLISHING

Hunter Publishing, Inc.
300 Raritan Center Parkway
Edison NJ 08818
Tel (908) 225 1900
Fax (908) 417 0482

ISBN 1-55650-721-6

Cover Photo: Mark Goebel

All photographs by the author except for
pages 123 & 127 (by Jeff Greenberg).

Other books in the camping series are
NEW ZEALAND, HAWAII, COASTAL CALIFORNIA.

Contents

INTRODUCTION   1

Geography   2
Climate   2
Experience   3
How To Use This Book   3
Choosing Your Campground   4
  • Florida's Commercial Campgrounds   6
  • KOA Kabins   6
  • Florida's State Parks   7
  • Florida's National Parks   9
  • Accessibility   9
  • Availability   9
  • Costs   10
  • Length Of Stay   10
  • Pets   11
  • Security   11
Becoming A Better Camper   12
  • Camping Terms   13
  • Renting An RV   15
  How Much Will It Cost?   16
  Packing Your RV Or Trailer   16
  • The Campsite   17
  • Camping Supplies   18
  • Insects   18
  Ticks & Lyme Disease   19
  Spiders   20
  • Reptiles   21
  Alligators   21
  Snakes   21
  • Plants   22
  • Sunburn   22
  • What To Take With You   22
  • Buying Or Renting Equipment   24
Recreation   24
  • Best Beaches   24
  Words of Warning   25
  • Golf   25
  • Tennis   25
  • Bird Watching   25
  • Hiking   26
  • Bicycling   26

- Canoeing   27
- Horseback Riding   27
- Spectator Sports   28
- Fishing   28
Fishing Licenses   29
- Diving & Snorkeling   30
Dangers Beneath the Waves   30
Camping Etiquette & Florida State Park Rules   32
Boating Safety   33

THE NORTHEAST   35

Amelia Island   37
- Fort Clinch State Park   37
Flagler Beach   39
- Bulow RV Resort Campground   39
- Gamble Rogers Memorial Rec. Area   41
Gainesville Area   42
- Gold Head Branch State Park   42
- Paynes Prairie State Preserve   44
High Springs   46
- O'Leno State Park   46
Jacksonville   47
- Flamingo Lake RV Resort   47
- KOA Jacksonville South/St. Augustine   48
- Little Talbot Island   50
Ocala   52
- KOA Ocala/Silver Springs   52
- Ocala Forest Campground   54
- Tomoka State Park   55
St. Augustine Area   56
- Anastasia State Recreation Area   56
- Bryn Mawr Ocean Resort   57
- Faver-Dykes State Park   59
- Marineland Camping Resort   60
- North Beach Camp Resort   62

THE PANHANDLE   65

Apalachicola   68
- St. George Island State Park   68
Bristol   70
- Torreya State Park   70
Chipley   72
- Falling Waters State Recreation Area   72

Dead Lakes   73
    • Dead Lakes Recreation Area   73
Destin   75
    • Emerald Coast RV Resort   75
    • Grayton Beach State Recreation Area   77
    • Holiday Travel Park   79
Lake Seminole   80
    • Three Rivers State Recreation Area   80
Marianna   82
    • Florida Caverns State Park   82
Old Town   83
    • Suwannee River KOA   83
Panacea & Sopchoppy   84
    • Alligator Point Campground   84
    • Ochlockonee River State Park   86
Panama City Beach   88
    • Panama City Beach KOA   88
    • St. Andrews State Recreation Area   90
Pensacola   92
    • Adventures Unlimited   92
    • Big Lagoon State Recreation Area   94
Port St. Joe   96
    • Cape San Blas Camping Resort   96
St. Joseph Peninsula   98
    • Rustic Sands Resort Campground   98
    • St. Joseph Peninsula State Park   100
Suwannee   102
    • Miller's Marine   102

CENTRAL EAST COAST   105

Cocoa Beach   107
    • Oceanus Mobile Village & RV Resort   107
Daytona Beach   108
    • Daytona Beach Campground   108
Fort Pierce   110
    • Road Runner Travel Resort   110
Jupiter   111
    • Juno Beach RV Resort   111
Melbourne   113
    • Sabastian Inlet State Recreation Area   113
Ormond Beach   115
    • Ocean Village Camper Resort   115
    • Sunshine Holiday Camper Resort   116
Titusville Area   118

- Great Outdoors RV Nature & Golf Resort   118
- Crystal Lake RV Park   120

CENTRAL WEST COAST   123

Bradenton   124
- Pleasant Lake RV Resort   124
- Horseshoe Cove RV Resort   126
Cedar Key   127
- Cedar Key RV Park   127
Dunedin   128
- Dunedin Beach Campground   128
Jennings   130
- Jennings Outdoor Resort   130
Leesburg   131
- Lake Griffin State Recreation Area   131
Live Oak   132
- Spirit of Suwannee   132
- Suwannee River State Park   134
Tampa & St. Petersburg   135
- Hillsborough River State Park   135
- Tampa E.Green Acres Camp/RV Park   136
Palm Harbor   138
- Clearwater Tarpon Springs KOA   138
Sarasota   140
- Myakka River State Park   140
- Oscar Scherer State Recreation Area   141

CENTRAL FLORIDA   145

Fort Mccoy   146
- Ocklawaha Canoe Outpost RV Park   146
Kissimmee   148
- Kissimmee/Orlando KOA   148
- Tropical Palms Resort   149
Lakeland   151
- Sanlan Ranch Campground   151
Lake Wales   153
- Lake Kissimmee State Park   153
Frostproof   154
- Camp Inn Resort   154
Orange City   156
- Blue Spring State Park   156
- Hontoon Island State Park   157
Orlando Area   159

- Yogi's Jellystone Park:Orlando/Kissimmee   159
- Wekiwa Springs State Park   160
Sebring   162
- Highlands Hammock State Park   162
Walt Disney World   164
- Disney's Fort Wilderness Resort/Camp   164
Winter Haven   165
- Holiday Travel Park   165

THE SOUTH   167

Fort Lauderdale   168
- Twin Lakes Travel Park   169
- Yacht Haven Park & Marina   170
Hobe Sound   172
- Jonathan Dickinson State Park   172
The Keys   174
- Big Pine Key Fishing Lodge   174
- Bahia Honda State Park   175
- Boyd's Key West Campground   177
- Fiesta Key Resort KOA   178
- John Pennekamp Coral Reef State Park   180
- Lazy Lakes Campground   182
- Long Key State Recreation Area   183
- Key Largo Kampground & Marina   184
- Sugarloaf Key Resort KOA   186
Miami   187
- Everglades/Homestead KOA   187
- Everglades National Park   188
- Miami North KOA   190
West Palm Beach   191
- Lion Country Safari KOA   191

THE SOUTHWEST & LOWER GULF COAST   193

Naples   195
- Collier Seminole State Park   195
- Crystal Lake RV Resort   197
- Naples/Marco Island KOA   198
Everglades City   200
- Barron River RV Park   200
Fort Myers   202
- Fort Myers/Pine Island KOA   202
- San Carlos RV Park   204
- Upriver Campground Resort   206

Introduction

The snows and storms of winter in the Northeastern United States usually mean one thing for the people who live there: escape. And escape they do, southward to the friendlier climes of Florida. The balmy breezes that blow across the state from one turquoise ocean to the other, the ever-present sunshine, and the wide sandy beaches have a magnetic attraction for the flocks of snowbirds that head southward from Canada, the American Midwest and New England. Each year, more than 41 million refugees from the icy regions of the north follow in the footsteps of Juan Ponce de Leon and head for Florida.

More people retire to Florida than to any other state. And now more than ever, Florida is fast becoming *THE* camping destination of the nation.

From Pensacola to Miami, from Jacksonville to Key West, there are more than 900 campgrounds. Some are large, spectacular resorts; some are barely big enough to accommodate a half-dozen RVs. Some are set on breathtaking seashores, some by the roadside at convenient locations chosen more for their accessibility than aesthetics. Some are operated by the state; a great many more are privately owned and operated; most are appealing in one way or another.

Appeal is, of course, subjective. What will often attract one visitor may repel another. Even so, there are certain minimum requirements, practical and aesthetic, that must be present for a campground to remain popular.

With so many campgrounds offering a range of facilities that varies from the barest essentials to an array of amenities and recreational opportunities, it has become increasingly difficult to distinguish between various classes of campgrounds, and almost impossible to identify the truly superior. Bearing in mind the cost and inconvenience of a poor choice, it's imperative that you pick the right campground. But how? This book will help.

The campgrounds listed throughout the following pages are those we consider the best in the state. They were chosen as much for the facilities and recreational opportunities they offer as for their geographical location and aesthetics. Security also was an important consideration.

Geography

Florida is a peninsula almost 450 miles long, 220 miles across at its widest point, tapering off to less than 100 miles at its narrowest. Beyond the mainland, a long ribbon of islands known as the Florida Keys curve gracefully westward from Miami into the Gulf of Mexico.

Florida is graced with more than 1,000 miles of beaches. From Pensacola, they border the Gulf of Mexico, the southern tip of the peninsula, and up the eastern shore to Jacksonville in the northeast. The land in between is a diverse mélange of urban development, wetland, forest, greenbelt, dunes, grasslands, sea grape and swamp, never rising more than a few feet above sea level and always bathed by the gentle tropical breezes and currents of the Gulf Stream. Only rarely, during the hurricane season, is the serene order of nature disturbed by heavy weather; even the rain is often pleasant and refreshing.

Climate

Florida is always warm, often hot, sometimes blistering. The daily highs averagein the low to mid-eighties, but it's not unusual for them to reach into the mid-90s in summer; rarely do they fall below the mid-50s.

The average rainfall is fairly even throughout the state at 53 inches per year, except in the Keys where it averages only 40 inches. June, July, August, and September are the months when the heaviest rainfall occurs.

The hurricane season is generally between June and November, with the peak occurring in September. Most likely areas to be hit by hurricanes are the Florida Keys, Miami, Naples, and the Gulf Coast of Northeast Florida, known as the Panhandle.

Experience

To those readers considering camping for the first time – those of you to whom the word "vacation" has always meant a king-sized room at a luxury hotel – you can rest assured that you will be pleasantly suprised. There's nothing quite like rising early in the morning, washing in the cool, clear waters of a woodland creek, and then eating breakfast cooked in the open air.

For the experienced camper – the outdoor family with the luxury RV and all the comforts of home on board – almost every entry in the following pages will have something that will appeal. You, as they say, have Florida's great outdoors at your feet.

How To Use This Book

This book is for campers of all levels of experience and expertise. Beginners and seasoned campers alike, with tents, trailers or RVs, will find a wealth of help and information.

For convenience, we have organized the state into seven geographic regions: The Northeast, The Panhandle, The Central West Coast, The Central East Coast, The Southwest, The Southeast and The South. Under each region is listed the best campgrounds organized under the particular city or town in which they are located.

Three types of campgrounds are listed: Commercial, State Park, and National Park. This is evident either when reading the name of the park or the entry itself. Each listing is preceded by a short description of the location, followed by a roundup of all the information, descriptive and practical, you'll need to make an educated choice.

The rest of the book will provide you with a wealth of practical camping information, do's and don'ts, and tourist information.

Choosing Your Campground

The success of your vacation depends on personal preferences. Make a bad choice and the quality of your vacation will go rapidly downhill; soon you'll be wanting to pull up the tent pegs and move on to find something better. Experienced campers know just how frustrating and costly that can be. There's nothing worse than heading down the road in search of the "Ideal Campground," knowing little of what might lie ahead. And, like a poker player, sure that a winning hand is only the next deal away, we are just as sure the ideal campground lies around the next bend. But, like the poker player's winning hand, it never seems to materialize.

It's a little disconcerting to look back over six or seven days of traveling the highways and backroads, wonder where the time has gone, and suddenly realize that yet another vacation has turned out to be less than you might have expected. A great vacation is guaranteed, however, if you can choose the right campground before you leave home.

This book provides a look at 100 of what we consider to be the best campgrounds in Florida. For many of the listings, the appeal will be obvious; for others, it will not be quite so apparent. From these listings you'll be able choose something that will appeal to *you*. Perhaps it will be a secluded oceanside location where you can get away from it all and spend some time alone with a loved one. Maybe you'll choose one of the oceanside resorts with lots of sea and sand and all the water sports that go along with them. Perhaps it will be one of the campgrounds located at the seat of the action in Miami, Orlando, or Tampa, close to the theme parks and attractions of Central or Southern Florida. How about a vacation in the wilderness? If that sounds appealing, you might choose to spend some time close to nature in one of Florida's state or national parks. Whatever your preference, there's something here to suit every camper.

Florida

Aside from the location and type of campground, you should also decide if you want to stay in one place, or perhaps visit several locations. To help you decide, you can make a checklist. Simply list the items that most appeal, and then browse through the book and pick out those locations that fulfill as many of the requirements as possible. Then it comes down to a simple choice of location.

Florida's Commercial Campgrounds

Profit is the motivating force at Florida's commercial campgrounds. Large or small, they're all in business to make money, and that's good for you, the camper. With more competition than many of them would like, the commercial campgrounds are constantly striving to improve facilities, services, and recreational opportunities. They are clean, tidy, and well cared for. Security in the smaller campgrounds is often non-existent, but it's taken much more seriously at the larger locations where gates are manned 24 hours a day and on-site personnel patrol the grounds.

Most of the larger campgrounds are self-sufficient, offering all sorts of amenities from laundries to full-service shops and stores, to marinas and restaurants. Some do not allow tents, catering only to campers with RVs or trailers. Many have rental units available: RVs, trailers, cabins, etc. Many more offer rental bicycles, boats, paddle boats, windsurfers, beach chairs and umbrellas. Larger campgrounds will have staff on hand to look after your needs around the clock, smaller ones might have staff available only for checking in during the daylight hours. Most will have a list of rules and regulations that restrict noise, pets, alcohol, and activities after dark.

KOA Kabins

These are rustic log cabins that provide some of the comforts of home and all the fun of camping out. Each cabin sleeps at least four persons, has an outdoor grill and picnic table, and campers have full use of the campground's amenities and services: hot showers, flush toilets, laundry, convenience store, and recreational facilities.

Florida's State Parks

Rarely considered by the camping community, some of Florida's state's parks offer facilities and recreational opportunities that rival those offered by many of their privately owned competitors, and will often offer some extra opportunities that the commercial grounds don't: group camping, youth camping, and primitive camping. And, as you might expect, camping at one of the state parks is almost always an outdoor experience where you can spend some time in the wilderness, on a deserted beach, or even far away from civilization on one of Florida's barrier islands.

The best of Florida's state parks – there are 38 we consider to rank at least as good or better than their commercial counterparts – you'll find listed, according to their geographic location, throughout the pages of this book.

Passes at state parks cost $3.25 per day per vehicle (maximum of eight people).

Hookups: Most state parks offer water and electric hookups (on individual campsites) for tent, trailer, and RV campers. Rest rooms and hot showers are conveniently accessible to all registered campers in these areas.

Group camping and youth camping is offered in designated areas for youth organizations, groups of families, or gatherings of friends. Facilities in group camping areas vary throughout the park system, from full-service cabins to limited accommodations.

Primitive camping is also available at many of Florida's natural communities. Overnight backpacking and canoeing into these areas is strictly for the physically fit, experienced, outdoor enthusiast.

Boat camping is offered at a few locations and usually includes mooring buoys, water and electric hookups, and the use of the park's campground facilities: restrooms/showers/bathhouses. While some parks do feature marinas, overnight camping at the slips is limited, so it's best that you check with the park staff for availability.

Cabins are for the camper who likes a roof overhead. Florida's state parks offer a variety of cabins in eight locations identified in the individual park listings. Some of the cabins feature the rustic appeal of the original Civilian Conservation Corps construction, while other contemporary cabins feature modern amenities.

Vacation cabins provide all the comforts of home, including private baths and kitchens. The facilities in these cabins vary from park to park, but typically sleep six, and may offer fireplaces and/or air conditioning.

Private cabins offer private sleeping quarters that are sometimes more convenient than other park facilities.

Group cabins are clusters of cabins, or large sleeping quarters. These group camps feature fully equipped kitchens, dining rooms, and/or meeting spaces.

Reservations for cabin rentals are accepted no more than one year in advance and a deposit equal to a two-night stay is required for a confirmed reservation. Calls for reservations should be made between 8 AM and 5 PM Monday through Friday.

Like camping fees, cabin rental fees vary from park to park according to season and the type of facilities offered, and are subject to change. Personal checks, Visa and Mastercard are accepted.

Added Attractions

Living History Programs: Many of Florida's state parks offer living history programs where visitors can learn what life might have been like for the Civil War Soldier or early pioneer.

Festivals and Events: The Florida Department of Natural Recourses offers a biannual publication highlighting the festivals, events, interpretive and environmental, and volunteer opportunities offered throughout the Florida State Park System. From turtle watching and a Camellia Christmas, to battle reenactments and environmental education workshops, "Festivals and Events" features all of these special occasions. You can pick up a copy at any Welcome Center or state park, or you can call (904) 488-9872.

Florida's National Parks

There are 35 campgrounds within Florida's three National Forests: Apalachicola, Ocala, and Osceola. Because facilities at most of the forest campgrounds are somewhat basic – no hookups, hand-pumped water, and so on – only a couple are listed here. If, however, you're one of those die-hard primitive campers, you may want to learn more about those that are not listed. You can obtain a booklet, "National Forests in Florida Recreation Areas Directory," to tell you more.

All three National Forests in Florida offer a wide range of hiking and backpacking opportunities, from short, interpretive trails to the long-distance Florida National Scenic Trail. The majority of the campgrounds are fairly small, but they are well kept, clean, and most are far away from Florida's busy highways and bustling cities. Fees are very reasonable and, if you don't mind roughing it a little, the National Forest campgrounds are a great value. Be sure to take all you need with you; service outlets can be miles away from your campground.

Accessibility

Most of Florida's campgrounds, state, national and commercial, are easily accessible. Only the more primitive areas inside some of the state and national parks require lengthy and often strenuous hikes. Campers going primitive should be sure they are in the best physical condition.

Availability

As Florida is rapidly becoming the premier camping destination in the United States, the availability of some sites can be a problem. Unless you book far enough in advance, this will effect not only where you camp, but when.

There really is no high season for camping in Florida. The most popular campgrounds stay pretty heavily booked from season to season. When the schools are out, and on most major holidays, especially Easter, Labor Day, and Christmas, it's almost impossible to find a site at any of the larger commercial grounds. And the choice sites at the state parks, allocated either by reservation or on a first come, first served basis, are almost always occupied. As the best campgrounds fill up first, those listed in this book are among the first to close their doors. If you're looking for a cabin, you should choose your location as far in advance as possible, and then book your reservation immediately; many are reserved up to a year in advance.

Costs

Commercial: Costs vary from campground to campground, ranging from $16 per night for a basic site with few frills to a high (depending very much upon location and time of year) of about $50 for a site with all the amenities, including private deck, table and chairs, beachside location and so on.

State Parks: Costs at state parks are much more predictable. You'll pay between $8 and $20 per night for your site, depending upon location and season. A waterfront site will cost you an extra $2 per night; use of the boat ramp will cost $2 to $4 more. Some of Florida's state parks have vacation cabins, all very much in keeping with the outdoor experience. These can cost, again depending on the location and the season, anywhere from $15 to $100 per night.

Camping fees for senior or disabled visitors are half the base cost.

Primitive camping costs $3 per person per night – $2 for those under 18.

National Parks: Rates vary from a low of $2 per vehicle at Apalachicola National Forest to a high of $8 at Osceola; camping in Ocala National Forest is free.

Credit Cards: Credit cards are accepted at most campgrounds throughout Florida. Those campgrounds that do not accept them will be identified within the individual listings.

Length Of Stay

Commercial: There are no restrictions at commercial campgrounds. You can visit for as long as you like, or for as long as you have money enough to pay the bill.

State Parks: Maximum of two weeks.

National Parks: 14 days in any one 30-day period.

Pets

Pets are not permitted in the camping areas at Florida's state parks, on the beaches, or in the concession facilities. Pets are welcome in national park campgrounds but must be kept quiet and on a leash. Pets are welcome at most commercial campgrounds. Check individual listings. It is unlawful in Florida to leave pets in a vehicle, locked or not.

Security

Most of the campgrounds listed in this book maintain good security and have the safety of their guests very much in mind, especially at the state parks. Theft, however, is always a problem. Leave your vehicle or camper unlocked, and you're liable to find your valuables missing when you return. The same goes if you leave your things lying around on the beach.

You're much more likely to find trouble on the roads than in the campgrounds. Car-jacking in Florida is an all-too-real problem. Keep your doors locked at all times when driving, especially at stop lights. At rest stops and welcome centers, keep a sharp lookout for suspicious characters; stay securely locked inside your car until they are gone, and then report them to the staff inside the facility. If you have a cellular phone, it's a good idea to keep it handy. Emergency 911 service is available almost everywhere.

Be careful inside public restrooms. Don't leave purses, pocketbooks, bags or any other tempting articles beside the washbasins. Snatch thieves are opportunists and move like lighting. Stay alert.

It's a good idea to invest in traveler's checks and leave jewelry at home.

Becoming A Better Camper

If you are not an experienced camper how do you become one? Where do you begin? The following tips will help you to get started.

Make your first camping trip a short one, say one or two nights, just to get the feel of it and to discover a pitfall or two. Go for a campsite that's fairly close to home; one that offers at least some of the basic amenities: hookups, showers, flush toilets, picnic table and grill rather than heading off into the wilderness. Be sure you book your site in advance.

Make new friends at the campsite, seasoned campers who can give you the benefit of their experiences.

Join a camping club. You'll find that fellow members will be pleased to offer help and advice to new campers.

If none of the above is available, buy a "how to" book and don't be afraid to take a chance and strike out on your own. There are many reliable books available at your local sporting or outdoor dealer.

Plan your trip, but try to keep things as simple as possible. Take only what you'll need. Plan meals: a menu for each day and pack your food supplies accordingly. With your menus in mind, be sure to pack the cooking utensils you'll need.

Divide cooking and cleanup responsibilities among family members and be sure to rotate duties on a daily basis; you don't want a mutiny on your hands.

Check weather forecasts. Florida can be hot and wet, but no matter where you go you should be prepared for extremes in temperature.

An RV is heavy on gas, so be careful how much weight you carry. For every 100 pounds of cargo you carry, you'll reduce fuel efficiency by 1%. Carry only enough food for the journey and buy your supplies when you arrive. Water weighs about eight pounds per gallon. If your vehicle has integral water tanks, carry only enough water to get you where you're going and fill up when you get there. Travel with the sewage tanks as low as possible, maintaining just enough so the chemicals to make it work.

Keep canned beverages in a separate cooler from your food supplies. Thirsty campers go to the well often. Opening and closing the unit can have an adverse effect on the efficiency of a food cooler. A small cooler will do fine for beverages, just refill it when it gets low; drinks chill quickly.

Take plenty of games and books – things for non-driving family members to do so they won't get bored along the way. Take a field guide to identify birds, plants and animals, and don't forget your camera.

Take it easy for at least the first 100 miles. If you've never driven a large vehicle or towed a trailer, you'll probably find it a somewhat harrowing experience, but you'll soon feel comfortable when you begin to get the hang of it. Remember to make wider turns. Practice reversing your trailer at home before you leave, rather than when you arrive at your campground where you're sure to have an interested audience.

If you're pulling a trailer, you'll probably need to make some slight adjustments so that the load pulls smoother. If your hitch weight is too light, the trailer will tend to fishtail. If it's too heavy, you might experience steering and braking problems.

When you return home, sit down and try to figure out what you've learned, and then commit your experiences to paper. Make additions or deletions to your check list.

Camping Terms

Absorption Refrigerator. A quiet, energy-saving way to keep food and beverages cold, though not as efficient as the domestic compressor type of refrigerator. Watch the temperatures on hot days. Don't put too many unchilled foods in the unit at once.

Black Water. The contents of your RV or trailer's flush toilet holding tank.

Camp Store. This is where you can always purchase bread, milk, and the basic essentials for living, but don't expect to find much in the way of fresh meat, fruit and vegetables.

Dump Station. Almost all the campgrounds listed in this book have dumping stations. Dumping was one of the criteria for inclusion. The dump station is where you empty your holding tanks. There's rarely a charge if you are staying on the property, but there might be if you are just stopping by to use the facility.

Gopher Hole. A homemade sewage outlet sometimes used in primitive camping areas. The concept is illegal except where specifically permitted.

Gray Water. Water from the RV or trailer's sink units and shower. It is stored in a separate tank away from the black water unit.

Hookups. Outlets for water, electricity, sewage, telephone and cable TV. The term "full hookups" means water, electricity and sewage.

Inverter. An on-board device used to convert 12-volt battery or generator power to 110-volt domestic power.

Pigtail. You may find that your electrical hookups are not compatible with those at your campground, in which case you will need to rent or borrow a compatible pigtail from the camp staff.

Pull-Throughs. Sites for those campers that aren't adept at reversing a trailer. You just drive straight on in, and then leave by driving out the other side.

Propane or LP Gas. Most outdoor cooking is done using this type of fuel. Most of the commercial campgrounds listed in this book can supply refills.

Recirculating Toilet. This type of unit recirculates flush water instead of using fresh water. A strong deodorant is used.

Sniffer. A gas detector which sounds an alarm when the presence of gasoline fumes, propane, or carbon monoxide is detected. Be aware that some smoke detectors and sniffers do not detect odorless carbon monoxide, which is deadly.

Renting An RV

Owning your own RV is, of course, the ultimate in camping pleas-
ure, but they don't come cheap and they are a lot work to equip,
clean, and maintain. Renting an RV, however, offers several advan-
tages. You can pick it up in one location and drop it off in another.
You can fly to your destination and pick it up when you get there,
thus saving yourself a long drive, giving yourself more time for
fun. When the trip is over, you can simply return it and let someone
else worry about cleaning it up.

Then again, should you consider buying an RV, you'll find renting
a good way to try out the various brands, types, and sizes. After all,
the purchase of an RV is a major investment. When you rent, you
can choose the type of RV that's best suited for that particular trip.
Best of all, when you rent an RV you rent a hotel on wheels and
freedom from schedules and suitcases. You can eat what you like,
when you like, and where you like.

The RV you choose to rent will always be something of a compro-
mise. Will you choose big and comfortable, or small and maneuver-
able? Will you go for economy of fuel, or decide to heck with the
expense and rent for luxury and all the comforts of home? Will you
rent from a local dealer, or will you book your RV by mail? If you
rent local, you'll be able to inspect your choices and book the one
that suits you best. If you do it by mail, you'll need to plan well
ahead, make some phone calls, and get some brochures.

If you're renting by mail, your brochures will display the floor
plans of the available vehicles. Don't be misled by how many
people a particular unit will sleep. Some bunks are suitable only for
children. Then again, if you're a very heavy person, an RV may not
be the best option for you.

A typical day on the road can mean breakfast of eggs and bacon in
the morning, eaten outdoors at a roadside picnic table, while
maybe watching the sun rise over the forest or ocean.

Lunch might be eaten miles on down highway – a plate of sand-
wiches, or a hunk of bread and butter with cheese and pickles. In
the afternoon you might take a little time out to visit a historical
site, or swim in the ocean, perhaps even a snooze, before hitting the
road and moving on again.

When you arrive at your campground, plug in to the water, electricity, sewer, telephone and cable TV, and then settle down to enjoy an evening with all the comforts of home. Not bad!

How Much Will It Cost?

You can rent a 15-foot trailer that will sleep four people for as little as $20 per day in the low season, $35 in the high season. Cruise America will, in the low season, rent you a 23-foot RV to sleep five people for $650 per week, including insurance. A 31-foot, top-of-the-line luxury motorhome that sleeps six will cost you $765 per week, including insurance. You will be required to leave a refundable deposit, depending upon the rental package you choose, of either $100 or $500. Cruise America has branches in most major cities throughout the country, including Atlanta, Orlando, Miami, West Palm Beach, and Tampa; you can contact them at (800) 327-7778. You will also be able to find local dealers in most major cities, Some will offer better terms if you pick up and return at the same location.

Other costs include campground fees that range from zero at some state and national parks to as much as $50 per night at Walt Disney World; the average is about $18. Fuel will be expensive: an RV will get four to eight miles per gallon, depending upon the size. Most rental companies charge a one-time cleaning fee.

Packing Your RV Or Trailer

There's nothing quite like heading out along the open road, totally relaxed, with nothing on your mind but fun and sunshine. And there's nothing quite so likely to destroy that feeling of euphoria than the frustration of trying to find a much needed item, only to realize it's buried deep among a huge pile of bits and pieces you've brought along with you, but might not even need. To ensure your good mood remains intact, you should take the time to pack your RV or camping trailer properly. The following tips will help.

First, know your limits. Your owner's manual will provide the recommended load limits for your RV or trailer. Most units, especially rental units, will have certification labels attached to the door jambs and trailer hitches. Don't ignore or abuse your limits. They have been calculated with your safety in mind.

Try to understand the principles of load distribution for your type of unit. If yours is an RV, ensure maximum stability by placing the heaviest cargo as far forward of the rear wheels as possible. Place heavy loads in the rear section and you'll have steering problems. If you're towing a trailer, place the heaviest load as close as you can to the area above its axle.

When loading your RV, try to place all heavy objects in the lower compartments between the axles to keep the center of gravity as low as possible. The same goes for trailers. Secure all heavy objects and try not to carry anything on the roof. Bicycles should be carried on proper racks, either at the front or the rear of the vehicle.

Place the items you will need most – food, beverages, clothing, personal items, cameras – where they can easily be reached. Make sure you close and secure all compartment doors before you move the vehicle. Take only one or two pots or pans and a minimum of cups and dishes (plastic or disposable cups and dishes if possible); learn to make do. The more you leave behind, the less work you'll have to do.

Be sure to take along an emergency kit, which should include a jack and lug wrench, flashlight, flares, tools, wheel blocks, at least two fire extinguishers, and a first aid kit. Keep one fire extinguisher up front and another in the kitchen area.

Finally, it's a good idea to draw a plan of your RV or trailer. Divide the plan into numbered sections, and then make a list of what is stored and where. Life gets a whole lot easier if you can easily find items when they are needed.

The Campsite

Your campsite will probably have a picnic table and a barbecue grill. Most of your cooking and eating will be done outdoors. When the temperature rises or drops drastically, however, you'll either close the door, fire up the a/c or heater, and cook and eat indoors. If not, you'll fire up the motor and head for the nearest restaurant.

Commercial campgrounds and resorts are a lot of fun for RV travellers. There's always lots to see and do, probably a pool, a recreation hall where you can dance or listen to live country music, a playground for the kids, and any number of outdoor games;

many offer planned activities under the supervision of a qualified staff member or recreation director. Many will be located close to a river, lake, or the ocean where you can fish, swim and go boating.

Most of the state and national park campgrounds offer less in the way of recreational activities, but prices are much lower. Some even offer amenities that commercial grounds don't: vast areas of forest, miles of unspoiled beaches, natural springs, historic sites, wilderness camping, primitive camping, interpretive programs, organized nature walks, canoe trips, and campfire programs.

Camping Supplies

These are easily obtained almost anywhere in Florida, except in heart of the Everglades, and even then you won't have to travel too far to obtain what you need. Many major campgrounds have large stores with an extensive range of groceries and camping supplies. State parks, however, rarely offer such luxuries. You can rest assured that wherever there's a state park campground, there will almost always be a commercial campground nearby, complete with a store and all the supplies you need. And even if there's not, there will be a gas station, grocery store, or shopping mall within a ten-mile drive.

Most commercial campgrounds can supply refills of LP gas, either by weight, meter, or both. Once again, state parks rarely offer LP service. And, while almost all commercial grounds offer sewage dumping services, state parks rarely do.

Ice is also a big consideration for campers, especially in Florida. It's a very profitable commodity for most commercial campgrounds, so it's always available. You'll find ice machines at some state park campgrounds, but that's the exception rather than the rule. Ice can be purchased at a nearby gas station.

Insects

All sorts of winged creatures are naturally attracted to Florida's flowers and foliage. Unfortunately, they will also be attracted to you. A pharmacist can advise you of any allergy medication or insect repellent you may require. Mosquito concentrations seem to be heaviest during summer months, especially during the evening hours. Wear a light-weight, long-sleeved shirt and pants along with your insect repellent and you should stay free of mosquitoes and other nighttime pests.

Other venomous insects you're likely to encounter are the fire ant, the honeybee, and the paper wasp scorpion. Only in cases where there's an allergy will emergency room treatment be required; calamine lotion will usually help ease the pain. More annoying than dangerous are the deerflies, inhabitants of shady wooded areas; black flies, in coastal areas; sand gnats, that make life on the beach just a little bit less than heavenly; chiggers, the little red bugs that inhabit the dense bushy areas in the summertime; and the horseflies, that live in the open woods and grasslands.

Ticks And Lyme Disease

Lyme disease is not the problem in Florida that it is in some other southern states. It is there, however, and anyone venturing into heavily wooded areas needs to be careful.

Lyme disease is a tick-borne viral infection for which there is no cure or vaccination. It need not, however, be fatal. A program of antibiotics will keep the disease in check until the immune system can build up antibodies to cope with it.

The symptoms of lyme disease are similar to many other illnesses: low grade fever, fatigue, head and body pain. The tick bite itself may at first go unnoticed, but, within a month of being bitten, a red rash may appear around the bite. Sometimes the rash is a solid red, sometimes it has a brighter outer edge with little or no color in the middle. Although the rash can vary in size from a point to where it can cover an entire arm or thigh, it usually is about four inches in diameter.

A blood test will usually confirm the disease by detecting antibodies in the immune system, but it can take as much as two months before those antibodies begin to appear.

The deer tick lives in wooded areas; that's where you're most likely to get bitten. Your pet may bring a tick to you. You can decrease the chances of getting bitten by doing the following:

- Use a spray, dip, powder, or collar to keep ticks off your pet
- Wear proper clothing when venturing into the forests or woodlands (long-sleeved shirts, long pants, and a hat)
- Use repellents
- Tuck your pants into high socks to keep ticks from crawling under your clothes
- Keep shoes and boots tightly laced
- Wear light-colored clothing (it will be easier to spot ticks before they can crawl into an open neck or button hole)
- Wear collared shirts
- Check your clothing after an outing

If you find a tick attached to your skin, don't try any of the old wives tales to remove it. The application of a lighted cigarette may cause it to regurgitate fluid back into your body, thus causing all sorts of infection.

Use fine-jawed tweezers and grip the tick as gently as possible, and as close to your skin as possible. Do not squeeze the tick's body or you will inject its fluids into the bite.

There are many good repellents on the market, but the strongest and most effective contain an agent called DEET. Of those with a DEET content of more than 50%, you could try Repel Sportsman, either in a pump spray or lotion; Repel Deerhunter, in a pump spray; and Muskol Ultra, in a spray can. There may be others by the time you read this. It is suggested that you use repellents with a DEET content of less than 20% for reasons of personal comfort. The chemical in strong concentrations can cause itching and burning.

Best of all are the proprietary brands of skin softener such as Avon's Skin-So-Soft, a product that was used extensively against all sorts of flying bugs and pests during the Gulf War. It smells nice and will not cause burning or itching.

Spiders

Watch out for the black widow spider; its bite can be dangerous. The black widow lives in old wooden buildings, on dead logs, wooden benches, and picnic tables. They are easily recognized by their jet black color, large bulbous body, and distinctive red hour-glass-shaped mark on their underside. If you are bitten, you should go immediately to an emergency room for treatment.

Reptiles

Alligators

The alligator is found throughout Florida and Southern Georgia. Alligators are not picky eaters and will attack almost anything that moves, including turtles, snakes, raccoons, fish, deer, other alligators and, of course, humans. It's rare for a year to go by in Florida without an alligator attack on a human. A couple of years ago a visitor disappeared while swimming in one of the northern rivers. Searchers found bits and pieces of body parts, all that remained of the adventurous one. Alligators often appear lazy and sluggish. In reality they are always on the alert and can move like lighting on land or in the water. The jaws of a full-grown alligator are extremely strong and can easily crush the shell of a large turtle. Males can grow to 11 or 12 feet, and specimens in excess of 17 feet are not unknown. A running alligator can easily reach a speed of more than 20 MPH.

If you swim in wilderness lakes and rivers, be sure to keep a sharp lookout. You might not be able to see a lurking 'gator, but you can bet he sees you. Never swim alone without a companion watching from the riverbank or lakeshore.

Snakes

The most dangerous poisonous snakes found in Florida are the coral snake, the pit vipers, the cottonmouth, and the eastern and pigmy diamondback rattlesnake. The copperhead and the canebrake rattlesnake are sometimes found only in northern Florida, but the diamondback is found statewide in dry areas. The pigmy rattler prefers a wet environment and is usually found near swamps, rivers, and lakes. The cottonmouth also likes the water and he too can be found in the swamps, on the riverbanks, and close to the lakes. The coral snake's environment is the upland, wooded areas of the state.

To avoid a snakebite, watch where you step; never put your hands into nooks and crannies or other rocky places; never go barefoot; sleep up off the ground.

If you or someone in your party is bitten, administer first aid (do not apply a tourniquet), and transport the victim immediately to the nearest hospital emergency room. If you are by yourself, go for help, but try to avoid exerting yourself.

Plants

There are some 60 poisonous plants in Florida. At least 15 of them, including some species of mushroom, are deadly if ingested; 25 more will cause nasty skin rashes.

To avoid problems, don't put anything in your mouth – not even if you're sure you know what it is. Don't touch plants you can't identify. Don't pick flowers.

Even the most experienced camper will sometimes fall victim to curiosity or misidentification. A victim of poisoning should quickly drink two or three glasses of water to dilute the poison, then vomiting should be induced – syrup of ipecac works well – and the victim transported to the nearest emergency room along with a sample of the poisonous plant.

Sunburn

As Florida is supposed to be the land of almost perpetual sunshine it's essential that you take a good sunscreen. Check with your pharmacist to ensure the proper SPF (sun protection factor) for your type of skin.

What To Take With You

CAMPING EQUIPMENT (Primitive Camping)

- Tent with a fly and a full set of pegs
- Ground tarp
- Air mattress or pad
- Sleeping bag

- Pillow and pillow case
- Backpack
- Compass
- Small first aid kit
- Map of the area
- Camp stove
- Portable grill
- Matches or lighter
- Coffee pot
- Cookware
- Dishes
- Eating utensils
- Plastic garbage bags
- Plastic self-sealing bags for food
- Dish towel
- ishwashing liquid
- Scouring pads
- Small ice chest
- Lantern/flashlight
- Hunting knife

CLOTHING

- Athletic or hiking shoes
- Sandals
- Cap or hat
- 1 or 2 long-sleeved shirts
- 1 or 2 short-sleeved shirts
- 4 pair socks
- 2 pair shorts
- 1 pair long pants
- Swimsuit
- Plastic poncho for rainy weather

PERSONAL ITEMS

- Toothbrush and paste
- Shaving cream and razor
- Feminine products
- Soap and shampoo
- Toilet and facial tissue
- Towel and washcloth

- Comb and brush
- Bug repellent for ticks and other insects
- Deodorant
- Sunscreen
- Sunglasses

Buying Or Renting Equipment

Perhaps you've never been camping before, don't have the necessary equipment, and certainly don't want to go to the expense of kitting up. Well don't worry, there's plenty here for you. Many of Florida's campgrounds offer rental tents, RVs, trailers, vacation cabins, and self-catering units. Some have restaurants on the property, and many of those that don't are close to communities that do. Then again, for a minimal outlay, you can purchase a small tent and a minimum of outdoor equipment and do it right. Major department stores such as Sears, K-Mart, and Wall-Mart carry a full range of equipment at reasonable prices; a small tent, 8' x 8' complete with fly, can be purchased for as little $49.95. If you like, you can rent all the equipment you'll need before you leave home. Many local outlets in your home town offer this type of service.

Recreation

Listed along with each campground you'll find some of the nearby attractions – historical sites, beaches, lakes, rivers, trails, state parks, theme parks, amusement parks, theaters, etc., all located within an easy drive of the campground of your choice.

Best Beaches

A survey to select the nation's Top 20 Beaches is conducted annually by the Laboratory for Coastal Control at the University of Maryland. Nine of these beaches are located in Florida's state parks. Rated on the natural quality of the beach, as well as the recreational value offered, each of the nine beaches are identified for you in the individual park listings.

Words of Warning

- Don't swim or surf on your own.
- Stay out of the water if you have an open cut or sore. Not only will you attract large predators, smaller fish will want a nibble, too.
- Stay out of the water during the hours of darkness.
- Stay out of the water if sharks are present.
- Try to swim or surf when there's a lifeguard on duty.
- Stay out of the water when the warning flags are flying.

Golf

One can't think of Florida without thinking of its magnificent golf courses, many of which are located close to the ocean in spectacular settings. Florida has more golf courses than any other state in the Union. Visitors can enjoy the sport at any number of excellent public and resort courses. You'll find those courses located close to campgrounds identified in the individual listings throughout the book.

Tennis

There are more than 7,700 tennis courts available for play throughout Florida, and courts are available on the property at many of the commercial and state campgrounds. You'll find them listed for you by individual campground.

Bird Watching

More than 450 species of wild birds make their homes in Florida. The state has about half of all bird species indigenous to the United States. Only two other states, California and Texas, can match Florida's bird population. Bird lovers can expect to see red-tailed and red-shouldered hawks, turkey vultures, northern bobwhites, red-bellied and downy woodpeckers, barred and eastern screech owls, red-winged blackbirds, egrets, herons, pelicans, gulls, willets, skimmers, terns, and a wide variety of warblers.

Birding is best done in the early morning. Find a spot and remain still and quiet. Be sure to take along your field guide, binoculars, and a notebook. The best times are said to be during the months April and May, and September and October. May is the best of all. For more specific information, contact the Florida Audubon Society.

Hiking

Hiking is a major pastime in Florida. Most of the state and national park systems have extensive hiking and nature trail systems for public use. The beaches also offer endless hiking opportunities, although this type of walking can be extremely strenuous and, because of the heat, is recommended only if you are in peak physical condition. Aside from the parks and beaches, Florida offers thousands of miles of foot trails leading through rolling pine forests, beside slow-moving rivers, and along hundreds of miles of country lanes and backroads. All are available for backpacking, birding, and nature watching. Many of the trails on public lands have been developed and are maintained by the Florida Trail Association. The Association's goal is to complete 1,300 miles of continuous hiking trails from Big Cypress National Preserve to Gulf Islands National Seashore.

If you get lost: First, don't panic; stay on the trail and don't wander into the woods. Second, conserve energy and food. If you can, climb a tree, look around and try to identify a landmark that will tell you where you are. Build a fire and make smoke to signal your position. Finally, if you must move, travel by compass in one direction only. Sooner or later you will reach civilization.

Bicycling

Bicycles are allowed on any roads normally open to motor vehicles. In addition, many of Florida's state and federal lands also have off-road bicycling trails. Others have scenic, paved, and dirt roads set aside for bicycles. Consult the individual park listings for details. Three park-to-park bicycle tours, from 101 to 327 miles, have already been developed by the Florida Park service. The service is determined to expand these routes throughout Florida. Contact the Office of Greenways and Trails.

Canoeing

Florida streams and rivers offer hundreds of miles of canoeing possibilities. Some have been designated State Canoe Trails, but these waters are also open to other users, including motorboaters. In most cases, though the waterways are publicly owned, the riverbanks belong to private individuals and are not open to public use. Canoe outposts throughout each region will equip you for a canoe trip, pick you up at your exit point, and shuttle you back to your car. In addition to the waterways in the state park system, the Florida Park service also administers some 36 canoe trails within the Florida Recreational Trails System for the more serious canoeist, ranging in length from four to almost 70 miles. While portions of this system do link with some of the state parks, most are publicly owned waterways which extend throughout the entire state, into National and State Forests, as well as county and city parks. The Florida Park service offers a Canoe Guide which describes all these trails, lists trail mileage, and offers a difficulty rating. For your copy of Florida Recreational Trail System/Canoe Trails, contact the Office of Greenways and Trails. For a complete listing of canoe outfitters, contact the Florida Association of Canoe Liveries and Outfitters.

Horseback Riding

Fifteen of Florida's state parks and all three national forests provide equestrian trails through some of the most scenic portions of Florida's state and federal lands. Several of these have staging areas or corrals and overnight camping for horses and riders. Please call the individual parks when planning your ride, organizing a group event, or to learn about trail conditions and any special regulations the park may have. Contact the Sunshine State Horse Council for information.

Note that proof of a recent negative Coggins test is required of all horses as they enter the park.

Spectator Sports

Florida is home to almost every spectator sport you can imagine from stock car and drag racing – at Daytona, Gainesville and Sebring – to major league football, baseball, basketball, and such obscure sports as jai alai. If you like variation, there's pari-mutuel sports which include greyhound racing, harness racing, and horse racing. Some 23 of the nation's major league ball teams hold spring training in Florida, and there are always collegiate sports to attend, including track and field, basketball, and any number of major college football bowl games.

Fishing

With more than 1,000 miles of available beaches, 7,700 lakes of 10 acres or more, more than 1,700 rivers and streams, and some 250 freshwater and saltwater species of fish, anglers often find themselves overwhelmed.

You can try your luck sportfishing in the deep waters of the Atlantic off Stuart, or any one of a many other locations on the East Coast. You can try the warm waters of the Gulf. Charters are available almost everywhere from Pensacola in the northwest all the way to Key West.

Perhaps the sailfish – Florida's state saltwater fish – is the most romantic of ocean catches, but the king of fish is, without doubt, the blue marlin. Catches of the "big blue" typically range from 100 to 300 pounds or more. Stories of four- and five-hundred pounders are not uncommon, and the stories of "the one that got away" tell of fish over 1,000 pounds. Flights of fancy? Maybe. The ocean is unpredictable.

Other excellent deep water catches include tuna, dolphin, tarpon, and kingfish, or king mackerel, which can be caught all year round, but fishing is at its peak during the spring and summer. There's wahoo, most often found lurking in the deep waters of the Atlantic, and amberjack, found in the cooler, deep waters just off the edge of the reef during the summer months and closer in the rest of the year. Amberjack can range in size from about 20 pounds to 40 pounds.

Sharks, too, are common in the waters of Florida: makos, blues, hammerheads, and tiger sharks abound. And, even though the encounter might be brief, your shark is sure to give you a fight to remember.

From the piers and beaches, anglers can cast into the surf for speckled trout, grunt, mullet, snapper, snook, striped bass, redfish, bluefish, drum, sheephead, flounder, whiting, pompano, and many more. If you like shellfish, you'll be happy to learn that Florida is known for them, including blue crabs, clams, oysters, scallops, shrimp, and stone crabs.

Freshwater anglers can hunt Florida's state freshwater fish, the largemouth black bass, the largest species of bass in the world.The black crappie, speckled perch, three species of catfish, the chain pickerel, also known as the pike or jackfish, the shellcracker, stumpknocker, warmouth, and the bluegill or bream can all be caught in Florida's waters.

Fishing Licenses

Florida saltwater and freshwater fishing licenses are required for all persons aged 16 and older. Some exceptions are provided by Florida law. The fees collected have been designated specifically for improving and restoring fish habitats, building artificial reefs, researching marine life and its habitat, tightening enforcement, and educating the public.

The Department of Natural Resources provides a pamphlet with exemption information, and one with size and species limit information. To get your copies of "Go Fish," and "Know Your Limits," contact: Department of Natural Resources, Office of Fisheries Management & Assistance Services, Mail Station #240, 3900 Commonwealth Blvd., Tallahassee, FL 32399-3000. (904) 922-4340.

To purchase a freshwater or saltwater fishing license, contact a county tax collector or visit a local bait or tackle shop. It's also a good idea to check for any specific local regulations that may be in effect at the time of your next fishing visit.

Diving & Snorkeling

Florida offers more opportunities for diving and snorkeling than any other state in the nation. Ocean and reef diving is available along the entire coast – east and west. The Keys are especially popular for diving. Lake and natural spring diving is available in 15 state parks. Snorkeling and scuba diving in rivers and springs is available year round, but periods of heavy rainfall sometimes cause flooding and make visibility a problem. Diving over reefs and from beaches is at its best when the winds are light, usually during the summer and fall.

There are more than 4,000 shipwrecks off the coast of Florida and dozens of certified dive operators will take you to explore them. They can also provide diving instruction, excursions, tours, and supply you with rental gear and valuable information.

There's an interesting monthly publication, *Florida Scuba News*, that presents dive information, directories, and equipment reviews. Contact the publisher at: 1324 Placid Place, Jacksonville, FL 32205, (904) 384-7336. Subscription is $14.25 per year.

The waters close to shore, both in the Gulf and the Atlantic, are often cloudy; visibility may be no more than a few yards. Farther out,the water is clear and visibility improves.

The waters of Florida's lakes and rivers can also be murky, but those of the sink holes and freshwater springs are very clear.

Dangers Beneath the Waves

It's taken for granted that experienced divers will know of the dangers. Beginning divers should be aware that the "deep" is most dangerous when you dive alone. Always go with a companion, or DON'T GO.

Always use dive flags when snorkeling or diving.

Always check local weather conditions, updated charts, and check with local dive operators.

Sharks are present in large numbers off both coasts. Smaller sharks are known to come inshore to a depth of as little as two feet. Rarely do they attack swimmers, but it does happen. Keeping this in mind, you should never go into the water if you have an open cut or scrape. Sharks can detect blood from a great distance.

Barracuda, found sometimes in the warmer waters of southern Florida and the Keys, are not really dangerous, just scary-looking, because of their rather frightening, ever-present grin. The barracuda is curious and will often follow you around.

Rays are not dangerous unless you happen to tread on one buried in the sand. If you do, you're probably in for a trip to the local hospital. The ray's first reaction is self-preservation. Its natural instinct is to lash out with that murderous tail. Unless he's threatened, the stingray is harmless and fascinating to watch as he flaps his way over the sandy bottom. Just watch where you're putting your feet.

Scorpionfish are also present in warmer waters to the south. They lie in wait for the unwary, on coral heads or close to the ocean floor. The fish has a set of thick spines on his back that can inflict a nasty sting.

The **stonefish** is often hard to see because of its camouflage, but he too can give you a nasty sting; be careful where you put your hand.

Jellyfish are transparent and often difficult to see. They inhabit the inshore waters everywhere; most are harmless. There are, however, some that are not. One is the Portuguese Man-o-War, prevalent both in the Gulf and the Atlantic. Avoid all jellyfish when possible.

Coral is found in quantity only south of Fort Lauderdale. It is often sharp and can cause cuts and abrasions. This is very painful. A delicate, living organism, coral is an endangered species in Florida's waters; don't handle it.

Sea urchins are the spiky little black balls that lie on the sandy ocean floor or in the nooks and crannies among the rocks. Their spines are brittle, often barbed, and will give you a very nasty sting. Fortunately, they are easily seen and avoided.

If you do happen to get stung by a scorpionfish, jellyfish, coral, or urchin, you can treat the sting first with vinegar to neutralize the stinging cells, and then visit the local drugstore where you can get something to ease the pain. Emergency hospital treatment might be necessary for a sting by a Portuguese Man-o-War or a stingray.

Camping Etiquette & Florida State Park Rules

Carry out your trash and dispose of it properly. Please bring extra trash bags to handle waste left behind by those less courteous than yourself. On the beaches, discarded fishing line, plastic six-pack containers and other refuse can maim and kill birds and other wildlife.

Don't feed the wild animals. If they become dependent on handouts they lose their natural fear of humans and can become aggressive, and even dangerous.

Don't approach wild animals. Use binoculars or a telephoto lens to extend your view. If you observe animals or birds exhibiting strange behavior, such as a broken wing, it's possible that you are too close. Move away slowly.

All native plants and animals are protected in state and federal parks. Leave them alone.

When hiking, try to stay on designated trails at all times. Cross sand dunes only where there are boardwalks. Most dune plants are protected because they help control erosion.

Help the sea turtles by not shining lights on them during the summer nights when they come ashore to nest and lay their eggs. Don't shine lights out to sea; you will confuse the turtles and they will crawl toward the lights instead of toward the ocean.

Firearms and alcohol are prohibited in state and national parks.

Try not to light fires; use a camp stove instead. If you must light one, use only dead and fallen wood.

Bury human waste in a hole at least six inches deep, away from running water and public water supplies, then cover it with dirt or a rock.

When bicycling, follow all traffic laws, communicate with and yield to hikers and equestrians. Stay on designated trails. Avoid riding when the trail is wet and don't skid on slopes and turns.

Anglers are encouraged to practice catch-and-release ethics.

Do not touch coral reefs. Coral is protected throughout the state. Use mooring buoys rather than anchors whenever possible; otherwise anchor on sandy bottoms only.

It is illegal to collect coral or tropical fish in state and federal parks.

It is illegal to injure or kill marine turtles, manta rays, porpoises, and manatees.

Do not approach, feed or touch manatees.

Boating Safety

Obey all boating regulations. Observe speed limits and motor restrictions when on the water, especially when traveling around other boats, swimmers and manatees, and over grass bottoms and fragile coral reefs.

Handle boat fuel and oil properly.

Clear water weeds from boats, motors and trailers immediately after returning to the ramp so that you won't spread them to other lakes and rivers.

Don't drink alcoholic beverages when on the water. Florida is winning the war against drinking on the water, and public opinion is steadily turning against it. Even so, more than 50% of all boating fatalities are alcohol-related.

Wear a life jacket. Lives would be saved if more people wore their life vests. Unfortunately, the age-old attitude that "it can't happen to me" still prevails and, alcohol-related or not, four out five deaths on the water are caused by drowning.

Federal law requires that every boat carry one personal flotation device (PFD) per passenger. Most inexperienced boaters don't realize that it only takes one unexpected wave or a waterlogged branch to throw them into the water. A bang on the head or the sudden shock of cold water will render a person helpless. Before the driver can turn the boat it's often too late; the unfortunate victim has become yet another boating statistic.

Manufacturers have come a long way in their quest to manufacture a more comfortable, better-looking life jacket. Some are now being made with specific activities in mind, such as water skiing or kayaking. These come in all sorts of colors and patterns and are lighter and more comfortable than the regular vests. Those made with the angler in mind now come with numerous pockets for tackle and lures.

The US Coast Guard has adopted several categories of life vest, some designed to automatically turn an unconscious person face up in the water. The following will help you decide which type will suit you best.

Flotation aid. A lightweight, more comfortable vest for use where help is never very far away. It's a popular pattern of life vest but will not necessarily turn an unconscious person face up.

Offshore life jacket. Best for open water and rough conditions when the wearer is likely to be in the water for an extended period. It's designed to turn an unconscious person face up. The jacket is a bit on the bulky side but it won't let you down.

Near-shore life jacket. Designed for use in calm weather and inland waters where help is close at hand. This type of jacket is comfortable but may not turn an unconscious victim face up.

Throwable device. Not recommended for use with children and non-swimmers. It could be a buoy, a boat cushion or a non-inflatable ring – anything that will keep people afloat provided they are physically able to hang on to it.

Special use devices. These are inflatables, or combinations of inflatable and permanent flotation. They are designed to provide the same buoyancy as offshore jackets, but are not as reliable. They are legal only for special use.

The Northeast

This is Florida's historic region. Jacksonville, with a population in excess of 600,000, is the largest city by area in the United States. The principle city in Florida's northeast region, St. Augustine, just 25 miles south of Jacksonville Beach, is the oldest city in the nation and the first permanent European settlement on the American mainland.

The coastal area of the region is a quiet, virtually unexplored outdoor destination of unspoiled beaches, secluded resorts, nature trails, bridleways, golf courses, lakes and rivers. You can fish, hike, and relax, never too far away from the attractions, and comforts of the big city.

Jacksonville is the commercial center for northeast Florida. Visitors are ferried across the historic St. Johns River to the city's 12-mile Riverwalk – a contemporary diversion of restaurants, shops and stores – and Jacksonville Landing, a waterfront marketplace with more than 120 retail outlets, shops and restaurants. This is the site of many local festivals and concerts.

Jacksonville offers plenty to see and do, from pristine Jacksonville Beach to Kingsley Plantation, home of a one-time slave trader who married an African princess. There is also the Anheuser-Busch brewery, Jacksonville Zoo, Mayport Naval Station, and a whole world of museums, art centers and historical sites.

Castillo De San Marcos, St. Augustine.

St.Augustine, founded some 42 years before Jamestown, is where visitors will find the oldest examples of almost everything: the oldest house, schoolhouse, store, jail, etc. Add a large number of cultural and historical attractions, several state recreation areas, and one of the finest beaches in Northern Florida, and you have a vacation destination like no other. These attractions include: the Spanish Quarter where St. Augustine celebrates more than 430 years of history; Castillo de San Marcos, a massive stone fortress built by the Spanish in 1672; Juan Ponce de Leon's so-called Fountain of Youth; the Mission of Nombre de Dios; and the St. Augustine Alligator Farm.

Gainesville, southwest of Jacksonville, is also a historical city. Here you can turn back the clock and visit the Morningside Nature Center where a 278-acre living history farm will let you sample

Castillo De San Marcos, St. Augustine.

what life in Florida must have been like more than a century ago. Outside the city, the small town of Micanopy has become a mecca for antique shoppers; the main street is lined with antique stores.

West of Jacksonville, the Osceola National Forest, is a sprawling, heavily forested wilderness that extends north from Lake City, through the Pinhook Swamp, Okefenokee Swamp Wildlife Refuge in Georgia. The entire : crammed with nature and canoe trails for outdoor enthusiasts.

For most of its length, the eastern coast of Florida is protected by a fringe of lonely barrier islands. Inhabited only by seabirds, the islands provide visitors with opportunities to get close to nature, hike the long sandy beaches, fish for a variety of saltwater species, ski, sail and scuba dive clear waters over limestone reefs and ledges.

Flagler County, south of St. Augustine, offers miles of virtually undiscovered beaches, tiny resort towns, and breathtaking views. Flagler Beach Pier is a must-stop for serious anglers.

Amelia Island

Fort Clinch State Park

2601 Atlantic Avenue, Fernandina Beach, FL 32034
(904) 261-4212

This park includes 1,121 acres at the north end of Amelia Island, Florida's northernmost barrier island. Fort Clinch offers a wide variety of sea island recreational opportunities beyond the popular tourist resort and residential areas of Amelia Island itself. The pristine beaches, unspoiled by the thousands that flee southward during the peak vacation periods, hold something for the entire family to enjoy, where the sun shines most of the time, and the kids can enjoy fun times in the sand.

Fort Clinch was named for General Duncan L. Clinch, an important figure in the Seminole War of the 1830s. The fort was constructed in 1847 and was occupied by a federal garrison during the Civil War. It was then taken over by Federal forces when General Robert E. Lee ordered a withdrawal in 1862. When the Civil War ended it was abandoned, but was reoccupied briefly in 1898 during the Spanish-American War. Today, the fort remains in remarkably good condition. Park rangers dress in Civil War Union uniforms and carry out the daily chores, cooking, sentry duty, and so forth, of a busy Civil War garrison. Candlelight tours can be arranged at the ranger station. There are annual reenactments during the months of May and October of the fort's occupation by Confederate and Union troops. The visitor center contains many exhibits, tools, utensils, and artifacts, which interpret the history of the fort.

FACILITIES: Coastal camping on 62 shaded, full-service campsites, complete with water and electric hookups, restrooms, hot showers, picnic tables, and grills. There's a primitive camp site for those who like to get a little closer to nature. The park has more than 8,000 feet of shoreline on the Cumberland Sound and 4,000 feet on the Atlantic Coast. There's also a picnic area for public use, a campfire circle, several hiking trails and fresh water showers at the beach. Snacks and soft drinks are available near the beach.

RULES & REGULATIONS: No pets, but guide dogs are welcome. Alcohol and firearms prohibited. Do not feed wild animals.

SECURITY: Very good. Round-the-clock security by a resident park manager. The gates are locked from sunset to 8 AM. Campers are provided with the combination to the gate lock, allowing free exit and access after the park has closed.

NEAREST SERVICES: The town of Fernandina Beach.

Downtown Fernandina Beach, Amelia Island.

RECREATION: Hiking the miles of nature trails or beach, swimming in the Atlantic Ocean, spending lazy days sunbathing. For the nature lover there's a wealth of wildlife to observe, including wading birds. Many species of marine birds and mammals make their homes in the hammocks and dunes on the east side of the park. Anglers can enjoy fishing from the beach or the pier on the Amelia River, the Cumberland Sound, or the Atlantic Ocean for speckled trout, striped bass, redfish, bluefish, drum, sheephead, flounder, whiting, and pompano.

NEARBY ATTRACTIONS: Amelia Island, Fort George, the Huguenot Historic Museum at Fort George. Little Talbot Island State Park and Fernandina Beach are just to the south, but north of Jacksonville. Guana River State Park, is south of Jacksonville, and there's a pari-mutuel dog track at Orange Park. Ponte Vedra Beach, the Fort Matanzas National Monument, and historic St. Augustine are all just to the south of Jacksonville on Highway A1A.

RATES: $12 per night October 1 through February 28; $17 per night March 1 through September 30.

OPEN: All year.

HOW TO GET THERE: From Fernandina Beach, take US A1A east. The park entrance is on the left.

Flagler Beach

Bulow RV Resort Campground

PO Box 1328, Flagler Beach, FL 32136
(904) 439-2549

The campground is just 10 minutes from the beach and good fishing sites. The pivotal points of interest are the nearby Bulow Plantation Ruins State Historic Site and the Bulow Creek State Park. Bulow once was a prosperous Southern plantation producing cotton, rice and indigo. What little remains of the once-proud estate tells the sad story of its fall as a result of the Second Seminole Indian War. Bulow Creek State Park was also a part of the great plantation. Of special interest is the 800-year-old Fairchild oak tree which, along with two water cisterns, has survived to become a monument of the people who pioneered the land and gave Florida its heritage. Today, Bulow Creek is a mecca for hikers and nature lovers. Several trails interlace the magnificent hammocks, which provide a natural habitat for a diversity of plant, animal, and bird life.

FACILITIES: More than 330 level, grassy, open and shaded sights – 250 with full hookups, 50 with water and electric only, 35 with no hookups; 100 pull-throughs. There are 26 rental cabins, as well as tents, canoes, and boats available. Telephone and cable TV hookups available (there's an extra charge for TV). The restrooms are clean, handicapped accessible, have flush toilets and hot showers. There's also a 6,000-square-foot recreation hall and civic center.

RULES & REGULATIONS: Pets are allowed if kept quiet and on a leash. Quiet time is 10 PM until 8 AM.

SECURITY: Good, but no gates. Security is handled by members of the local police department who patrol the grounds.

NEAREST SERVICES: On the property. There's a restaurant, a full-service store with ice available, RV supplies, LP gas refills by weight and meter, gasoline available, laundry room, public phone, sewage dumping station, tables, fire rings, and wood.

RECREATION: Swimming in the giant pool; hiking and nature watching at the nearby state parks; sunning, swimming, fishing, boating, sailing, windsurfing on the beach; lake and river fishing; watching top-name entertainment at the on-site civic center; basketball, shuffleboard, volleyball, badminton; planned group activities by resort staff. There's also a large playground for the kids.

NEARBY ATTRACTIONS: Bulow Plantation Ruins State Historic Site, Bulow Creek State Park, Ormond Beach, Daytona Beach, the International Speedway, Flagler Beach, Flagler College, Faver-

Dykes State Park, Marineland of Florida, the Gamble Rogers Memorial State Recreation Area, and the Fort Matanzas National Monument, New Smyrna Beach, the Canaveral National Seashore and the Kennedy Space Center are south beyond Daytona Beach.

Flagler College, St. Augustine.

RATES: $18.50 per day.

OPEN: All year round. Reservations recommended November 1st through April 1st.

HOW TO GET THERE: From Jacksonville, take I-95 to Exit 91 and Highway 100. From Daytona Beach go north on I-95 to Exit 91. From Exit 91, go a ¼ mile east on Highway 100, then three miles south on Old Kings Road.

Gamble Rogers Memorial Recreation Area

3100 South A1A, Flagler Beach, FL 32136
(904) 439-2474

Gamble Rogers is bordered by the Atlantic on one side and the Intracoastal Waterway on the other. The 144-acre park offers a quiet place to spend time sun bathing while the kids enjoy themselves in the water. Its a place for bird watching, chasing the tiny crabs as they bury themselves in the sand, or watching the sea turtles in the summer months when they come ashore to lay their eggs.

FACILITIES: Coastal camping on modern, full-service campsites with water and electric hookups. Restrooms, hot showers, picnic tables, and grills. There's also a picnic area, and a boat ramp.

RULES & REGULATIONS: No pets, but guide dogs are welcome.

SECURITY: Good. Round-the-clock security by a resident park manager. The gates are locked from sunset to 8 AM. Campers are provided with the combination to the gate lock, allowing free exit and access after the park has closed.

NEAREST SERVICES: Less than a ½ mile away in Flagler Beach.

RECREATION: Hiking along the beachfront; fishing in the surf for sea trout, bluefish, pompano, whiting, redfish and flounder; nature study, picnicking, swimming, and boating.

NEARBY ATTRACTIONS: The Pellicer Creek Canoe Trail is at Faver-Dykes State Park; Historic St. Augustine is about 35 miles to the north on Highway A1A, while Bulow Creek State Park, Bulow Plantation Ruins State Historic Site, Ormond Beach, Flagler Beach,

Plantation Ruins State Historic Site, Ormond Beach, Flagler Beach, Marineland of Florida, the Fort Matanzas National Monument, Daytona Beach and the International Speedway are all nearby. Sugar Mill Gardens, New Smyrna Beach and Sugar Mill Ruins State Historic Site, the Canaveral National Seashore and the Kennedy Space Center are all just a little farther down the coast to the south.

RATES: $8 per night.

OPEN: All year.

HOW TO GET THERE: Take A1A going south from Flagler Beach, or north from Daytona Beach. The park is in Flagler Beach off A1A.

Gainesville Area

Gold Head Branch State Park

3100 South A1A, Flagler Beach, FL 32136
(904) 439-2474

This park offers the casual vacationer something just a little different, a little more secluded, definitely more relaxing, and perhaps much more interesting than the usual hustle and bustle of Florida's conventional seaside vacation hot-spots. The 1,562-acre park is an area known as the Central Ridge. It's pretty remote (six miles from the nearest community) and set among rolling sandhills, marshes, lakes, and cleft by a deep ravine. It's overflowing with wildlife and offers a variety of outdoor activities for all the family. While the park itself is fairly large, the campground is quite small.

FACILITIES: Three separate areas contain 74 campsites with water and electric hookups; all have picnic tables and grills. The restrooms are handicapped accessible; the bathhouse has flush toilets and hot showers. There are 14 fully furnished rental cabins complete with all modern conveniences, and there's a primitive campsite for those hardy types who like to "rough it." There's also a youth camping facility for use by non-profit organizations. Sewage disposal is available for overnight campers only.

RULES & REGULATIONS: No pets, but guide dogs are welcome. Alcohol and firearms prohibited. Do not feed wild animals.

SECURITY: Very good. Round-the-clock security by a resident park manager. The gates are locked from sunset to 8 AM. Campers are provided with the combination to the gate lock, allowing free exit and access after the park has closed.

NEAREST SERVICES: There's a concession stand, vending machines, and an ice machine on the property, but the nearest grocery store is six miles away in Keystone Heights.

RECREATION: There are several lakes on the property – in fact, the park is completely surrounded by more than a hundred lakes. The lakes, in conjunction with Gold Head Branch, provide all sorts of water activities: swimming, fishing, canoeing, etc. A public boat ramp provides access to Lake Johnson, and another to Sand Hill Lake, to the west. There's a public swimming area for campers on Little Lake Johnson. Other recreational facilities include a campfire circle, a bicycling trail, and a picnic area. Rental canoes and bicycles are available, too. The fishing, both on Lake Johnson and Gold Head Branch is excellent: largemouth bass, bream, shellcracker, and speckled perch.

For hikers, there are four marked trails within the park. The Florida Trail is a two-hour hike, recommended only for experienced hikers. It begins at the park entrance and winds its way through the park's high country. The Ravine Ridge follows along the ravine from the stairway to the mill site. The Loblolly Trail is a loop trail that begins and ends at the mill site, and includes the largest loblolly pines in the park along the way. The shortest trail is the Fern Loop. It starts at the ravine stairway and passes by the head springs of the Gold Head Branch.

RATES: $10 per night. The rate for rental cabins from March through September is $40; October through February, $35.

OPEN: Year round.

HOW TO GET THERE: The park is six miles northeast of Keystone Heights. From the junction of Highways 21 and 100, drive six miles northeast on Highway 21.

Paynes Prairie State Preserve

Route 2, Box 41, Micanopy, FL 32667
(904) 466-3397

Paynes Prairie is a 19,000-acre preserve in one of Florida's historically significant areas. Within its boundaries are some 20 distinct biological communities that provide habitats for a wide variety of wildlife and birds. The preserve is still one of the state's best kept secrets and is, as of yet, an undiscovered recreational paradise. Although the park is one of the largest in the state, the campground is quite small, lovingly maintained, and kept immaculately clean.

FACILITIES: Of the 50 available sites, 35 are for RVs or trailers and have water and electric hookups, picnic tables, and grills. There are 15 more tent sites without hookups. The restrooms and bathhouse, have hot showers and flush toilets, andare handicapped accessible. Sewage disposal is available for overnight campers only. There are a number of public telephones on the property.

RULES & REGULATIONS: No pets, but guide dogs are welcome. Alcohol and firearms prohibited. Do not feed wild animals. Stay away from the bison, wild horses, and alligators. They are extremely dangerous.

SECURITY: Very good. Round-the-clock security by a resident park manager. The gates are locked from sunset to 8 AM. Campers are provided with the combination to the gate lock, allowing free exit and access after the park has closed.

NEAREST SERVICES: Less than three miles away in Micanopy, or 10 miles to the north in Gainesville.

RECREATION: There's a picnic area with grills, tables, several shelters, and restrooms in the Lake Wauberg recreation area. Nature lovers will enjoy Paynes Prairie for the excellent bird and nature watching opportunities. You can expect to see sandhill cranes, eagles, hawks, a wide variety of waterfowl and wading birds, wild horses, bison, alligators, otters, and many other species of marine life. Other activities you might enjoy include bicycling on a half-dozen designated trails, hiking along several trails of varying length and difficulty, horseback riding on two trails, one more than six miles long, and canoeing. Park service rangers conduct a program of weekend guided walks and backpacking hikes from

October through March. You can call (904) 466-4100 for details. The fishing is excellent: largemouth and smallmouth bass, bluegill, shellcracker, bream, etc. There's a boat ramp for small boats with electric motors only, canoes, and sailboats.

NEARBY ATTRACTIONS: Devil's Millhopper Geological Site, at 4732 Millhopper Road in Gainesville, is a huge sink hole that has fascinated people as far back as the early 1880s. Water from tiny streams tumbles 120 feet down the steep sides of the basin to disappear through the cracks and crevices into the unknown. The 6,500-acre San Felesco Hammock State Preserve is four miles to the northwest of Gainesville on Highway 232. The Fred Bear Museum, at I-75 and Archer Road in Gainesville, dedicated to the world of archery, is an educational experience for all ages. Admission is under $5; (904) 376-2411. The Florida Museum of Natural History on Museum Road is ranked one of the top 10 natural history museums in the country; open Tuesday through Saturday 10 AM until 5 PM, and Sunday 1 to 5 PM; admission is free; (904) 392-1721. The Marjorie Kinnan Rawlings State Historical Site, is just to the southwest of Gainesville near Hawthorn. It's one of Florida's most popular attractions. The cracker-style home is where the author wrote her prize-winning novel, *The Yearling*; open Thursday through Monday from 10 AM until 11:30 AM, and 1 until 4:30 PM; closed Tuesday and Wednesday.

RATES: June through September, $8 per night. October through May, $10 per night.

OPEN: The campground is open year-round. The visitor center is open from 9 AM until 5 PM. daily, and displays a variety of exhibits, along with an audio visual program that interprets the preserve, its culture and natural history.

HOW TO GET THERE: The preserve is 10 miles south of Gaines-ville. From the junction of Highways 121 and 441, drive south for 10 miles on 441.

High Springs

O'Leno State Park

Route 2, Box 1010, High Springs, FL 32643
(904) 454-1853

Hardwood hammocks, sink holes, a river swamp, and a sandhill community all go toward the making of one of the oldest of Florida's state parks. It was developed in the early 1930s by the Civilian Conservation Corps. The Corps' suspension bridge, one of the park's unique features, still spans the river. O'Leno is nestled on the banks of the scenic Santa Fe River. The river, a tributary of the Suwannee, enters the park only to disappear into one of the several sinkholes. It then flows underground for several miles before appearing again. The campground is medium-sized with extensive family, group, and youth camping facilities and great opportunities for outdoor recreation.

FACILITIES: Of the 60 sites, all have water and electric hookups, picnic tables and grills. The restrooms are handicapped accessible, and the bathhouse has flush toilets and hot showers. The group camp can accommodate up to 140 persons in 18 cabins (available with cots and mattresses, but no pillows or bed linens). The kitchen and dining hall are fully equipped with cooking utensils, dishes, and flatware. There's also a meeting room and a pavilion. Primitive campsites are available for those who like to rough it.

RULES & REGULATIONS: No pets, but guide dogs are welcome. Alcohol and firearms prohibited. Do not feed wild animals.

SECURITY: Very good. Round-the-clock security by a resident park manager. The gates are locked from sunset to 8 AM. Campers are provided with the combination to the gate lock, allowing free exit and access after the park has closed.

NEAREST SERVICES: There's a general store on the property where you can buy some of the necessities, as well as a variety of locally made crafts and gifts. The nearest full-service supermarket is about six miles away in High Springs, where you'll also find a few family-style restaurants.

RECREATION: As with most state parks in Florida, so it is here at O'Leno. Hiking, backpacking, nature study, fishing, swimming, canoeing, and horseback riding are the popular pastimes. For hikers, there are two scenic nature trails: the Santa Fe Trail which follows the river bank to the sinkhole where the river disappears underground, and the Limestone Trail, a shorter but very scenic walk. Nature lovers may spot alligators, turtles, and a wide range of wildlife and birds. Anglers will find the fishing excellent; largemouth bass, bream, shellcracker and catfish abound in the Santa Fe.

NEARBY ATTRACTIONS: Olustee Battlefield State Historic Site is just a few miles to the northeast off Interstate 10; Ichetucknee Springs State Park is nearby off Highway 41; Lake City is about 20 miles to the north on Interstate 75; the Ocala National Forest stretches away to the east. The Stephen Foster Memorial and the Old Telford Hotel, where Chuck Harder broadcasts the "For The People" radio talk show, are at White Springs to the north of Lake City on Interstate 10; the Stephen Foster State Folk Culture Center is also in White Springs.

RATES: $10 per night.

OPEN: Year round.

HOW TO GET THERE: The park is located on US Highway 441, six miles north of High Springs. From the junction of Interstate 10 and Highway 441, drive south for 20 miles on 441.

Jacksonville

Flamingo Lake RV Resort

3640 Newcomb Road, Jacksonville, FL 32218-1510
(800) 782-4323

This is a small, fairly new campground of about 50 acres with a 17-acre lake and a sandy beach just to the northwest of Jacksonville.

FACILITIES: Lakeside camping on 80 wooded and open sites: 30 are pull-throughs, 55 have full hookups to 30 amps, tables, cable

TV, public phone; 15 more have water and electric only; 10 have no hookups at all. The bathhouse is a class act: clean, and well-appointed with hot showers and flush toilets. There's also a nicely equipped laundry room, public telephones, and a sewage dumping station.

RULES & REGULATIONS: No large dogs unless you are staying by the month. Small dogs are permitted if kept on a leash. Quiet time is from 10 PM until 8 AM.

SECURITY: Quite good. No gates. Security by regular on-site patrols.

NEAREST SERVICES: On the property. There's a store where you can purchase groceries, paper goods, gifts, camping supplies, and ice; LP gas is available by weight and meter.

RECREATION: Fishing, boating, and swimming in the lake. Sightseeing in and around Jacksonville.

RATES: $22 per day; $120 per week.

OPEN: All year.

HOW TO GET THERE: Take I-295 west from I-95, or north from I-10, to Lem Turner Exit 13. If traveling north, turn left; going south, turn right.

KOA Jacksonville South/St. Augustine

9950 KOA Road, St. Augustine, FL 32095
(904) 824-8309

Here you can enjoy scenic waterside camping on large, shady sites in a pine forest. The sites are located on the edge of a 10-acre lake, not too far from the excitement and attractions of the nearby resorts of Jacksonville Beach and St. Augustine. The campground is small enough to maintain an intimate, family atmosphere, but can get very busy at times.

FACILITIES: Of the 110 sites, 62 have full-service hookups to 30 amps, 48 have water and electric only, and 62 are pull-throughs. There are Kamping Kabins and group sites for tents, and rental

tents are also available. The well-kept ba
plenty of hot water for the showers, even late

RULES & REGULATIONS: Pets are allowed if
leash, and you pick up after them. The quiet time
until 7 AM.

SECURITY: Quite good. No gates, but the campground is
constant surveillance by resident managers and staff.

NEAREST SERVICES: On the property. There's a full-service store
where campers can purchase groceries, RV and camping supplies,
LP gas by weight and meter, and ice.

RECREATION: There's a large recreation room and pavilion, a
spacious swimming pool with furniture, a game room with coin-
operated games, and rental pedal boats and canoes. You can go lake
fishing and swimming, play mini-golf, basketball and horseshoes,
and there's a nice playground for the kids. Planned group activities
organized by qualified members of the staff (tours, etc) are available during the winter months.

The Jacksonville skyline.

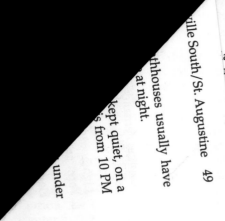

a Island State Recreation Area,
ienot Historic Museum at Fort
River State Park, Little Talbot
invville itself, and the Mayport
Castillo de San Marcos, the
ne, and the famous Alligator
ie. There's a pari-mutuel dog
tanzas National Monument,
Gardens, Fernandina Harbor
idina Beach, Marineland of
id the Morningside Nature
0-minute drive of the camp-

RATES: $24 per day for two people; $3 extra per person per day.

OPEN: Year round.

HOW TO GET THERE: From the junction of I-95 and I-10, go south on I-95 for 20 miles to Highway 210. Go one block east on Highway 210.

Little Talbot Island

11435 Fort George Road East, Fort George, FL 32226
(904) 251-2320

Little Talbot Island State Park is another unique sea island in northeastern Florida. The park encompasses more than 2,500 acres and over five miles of glistening, sandy beaches. It's a picturesque, undisturbed hammock of sand dunes and troughs covered with live oak, southern magnolia, American holly, sea oats, and morning glories. During the fall and spring months, a variety of migrating birds stop off to enjoy this remote island.

Nature lovers will enjoy wandering the dunes and forests, observing the abundance of animal and bird life. River otters, marsh rabbits, bobcats, and a variety of sea and shore birds inhabit the island. It's an ideal spot for birding.

Little Talbot boasts one of the nation's "Top 20 Best Beaches," so it's no surprise that the island, still largely undiscovered, offers some of the best swimming, surfing, and sun bathing anywhere in the United States.

FACILITIES: Coastal camping on modern, full-service campsites, among the hammocks. Water and electric hookups, restrooms, hot showers, picnic tables, and grills. Rental bicycles and canoes. Sewage dumping station. There's also a picnic area for public use. Youth camping facilities are available. Most facilities are handicapped accessible.

NEAREST SERVICES: About 17 miles either to the north at Fernandina Beach, or south in Jacksonville. There are two nice restaurants about three miles to the south – the Buccaneer and Peppers.There's a Little Champ convenience store, also three miles to the south, where you can buy some basic necessities, including gas (expensive). Stock up before you arrive. Bring your own wood.

RULES & REGULATIONS: No pets, but guide dogs are welcome. Quiet time 10 PM until 8 AM.

SECURITY: Excellent. Round-the-clock security by on-site staff and a resident park manager. The gates are locked 24 hours a day, which can be a bit of a nuisance, but provides a real sense of security. Campers are given the combination to the gate lock.

ACTIVITIES: Canoe trails interlace the salt marshes, rivers, and creeks. There's also hiking on the beaches, bicycling the trails through the hammocks and marshes, sunbathing, surfing, and swimming in the Atlantic Ocean, nature study, bird watching – there are 180 species of birds in residence – and wildlife photography. There is also plenty of fishing in the surf, marshes, river, and creeks.

OPEN: Year round.

RATES: $15.75 for basic site without hookups; $17.88 for site with water and electric hookup. Canoe rental $3 per hour; bicycle rental $2 per hour.

HOW TO GET THERE: Little Talbot Island State Park is 17 miles northeast of downtown Jacksonville. From the junction of I-95 and Highway 105, go 14 miles east on Highway 105, then three miles north on Highway A1A.

Ocala

Ocala is a small city set right in the heart of central Florida. It's an area surrounded by the great outdoors, and consequently offers wonderful opportunities for recreation. The Ocala National Forest stretches east, north, and south, and it too, offers a number of outstanding opportunities.

KOA Ocala/Silver Springs

3200 SW 38th Avenue, Ocala, FL 34474
(904) 237-2138

A nice, modern campground with lots of facilities in a spacious, woodland setting. Huge oak trees, magnolias, duck ponds and ornamental lakes with waterfalls and rock gardens surround the camping area. It's close to the Silver Springs Theme Park, horse farms, and the shops in Ocala.

Silver Springs, the centerpiece attraction for the area, discharges more than 64 million gallons of water a day, and is the headwater of the Silver River. The entire region is one of great natural beauty, ideal for nature lovers, bird watchers, and photographers. The campground is large; the sites, set among huge oaks and magnolias are shady, spacious, and well-maintained.

FACILITIES: Of the 300 sites, 127 have full-service hookups, 173 have water and electric hookups, all to 30 amps; 150 are pull-throughs. There are also a number of one-room Kamping Kabins and tents available for rent. The bathhouses and restrooms are clean and well-maintained, and there is hot water for the showers around the clock. The laundry room is equipped with modern machines and kept in tip-top condition. Sewage disposal is available for overnight campers only; cable TV carries an extra charge; and there are public telephones within easy reach of most sites.

RECREATION: There's a large recreation hall, a heated swimming pool with lots of room and pool furniture, a hot tub and a sauna. All the usual court games are available, and there's a playground for the kids. For the adults there is a large clubhouse with a meeting room and lounge. You may rent pedal boats, go hiking, biking, boating, canoeing, horseback riding, or picnicking at any one of many nearby state and national parks. The staff offers a full program of planned group activities and tours during the winter months. Silver Springs and the surrounding forest is fishing country. There are at least 50 lakes nearby, including Lakes George and Orange, all well-stocked with largemouth, smallmouth, striped and sunshine bass, shellcracker, warmouth, stumpknocker, bluegill, redbreast sunfish, crappie and catfish. There are as many public access boat ramps as there are lakes. If you're a golfer, you won't have too far to go to enjoy a challenging round. The Ocala Municipal Golf Club is just two miles away.

RULES & REGULATIONS: Pets are welcome. Quiet time is 10 PM until 7 AM.

SECURITY: Good. No gates, but there is a resident staff to keep an eye on things. Keep vehicles and trailers locked at all times.

NEAREST SERVICES: On site full-service store, LP gas by meter or weight, and ice. There are grocery stores and restaurants less than a ½ mile away.

NEARBY ATTRACTIONS: In Silver Springs there's the Early American Museum, Wild Waters Theme Park, and Silver Springs Theme Park. In Ocala there's Jai-Alai and the Reptile Institute. Paynes Prairie State Preserve, Lake Catherine, Half-moon Lake, Lake George, Devil's Millhopper Geological Site, San Felesco Hammock State Preserve, Newman's Lake, Orange Lake, Marjorie Kinnan Rawlings State Historical Site, and the Ocala National Forest are all within a short drive of the park. Walt Disney World, EPCOT, Sea World, and Universal Studios are 70 miles south on Highway 27.

OPEN: Year round.

RATES: Full-service sites, $22 daily for two adults. Additional adults $5 extra, per person, per night; children 4 to 17, $3 extra per person, per night; children under 4 free. Kamping Kabins $25 per night for two adults. For extra persons, see above.

HOW TO GET THERE: From the junction of I-75 and Highway 200 (Exit 68), go west for 75 yards on Highway 200, and then north on 38th Avenue for about a ½ mile.

Ocala Forest Campground

26301 SE City Highway 42, Umatilla, FL 32784
(904) 669-3888

This is a very attractive, secluded waterside campground on the shores of Lake Dorr at the southern edge of the Ocala National Forest. Just to the east of Lake City, the 430,000-acre forest is a huge tract of well-developed national recreation area. Natural habitats of longleaf and slash pine woods, cypress and bay swamps, numerous lakes, rivers and creeks are common attractions. This park is the focal point of Florida's "Ridge Country." The campground is small enough to maintain its individuality and provide an intimate family atmosphere. The management and staff are very involved.

FACILITIES: Of the 120 sites, 95 have full-service hookups to 30 amps, 30 have water and electricity only; 56 are pull-throughs. Rental RVs and tents are available. The bathhouse is large, clean, well-maintained, and has flush toilets and hot showers. The laundry room is equipped with modern machines; there are public phones handy to most sites. Sewage disposal is available to overnight campers.

SECURITY: Quite good. No gates. Security provided by on-site staff.

NEAREST SERVICES: On the property: there's a full-service store where you can purchase groceries, paper goods, camping supplies, ice and LP gas refills by meter. The nearest grocery store and restaurant is about seven miles away in Umatilla.

RULES AND REGULATIONS: Pets welcome if kept on a leash. No rowdy behavior. The quiet time is 10 PM until 7 PM.

RECREATION: The campground has a large recreation hall, heated swimming pool, playground, and all the usual court games. There's also a boat dock and ramp. You can rent row boats and bicycles. Hiking, backpacking, bicycling and horseback riding is available along the trails and bridleways of the forest, along the shores of the lake, and on a 20-mile section of the National Scenic Trail. You can go fishing, boating and canoeing on the lake and small nearby streams. Birding and nature watching in the freshwater marshes, swamps and flatwoods are available. There are planned activities during the winter months.

RATES: $95 for the week,

OPEN: All year.

HOW TO GET THERE: From the jun
at Altoona, go five miles west on Highwa

Tomoka State Park

2099 North Beach Street, Ormond Beach, FL 32174
(904) 676-4050

Tomoka State Park is near the junction of the Tomoka and Halifax rivers. Although it offers scenic beauty, creeks, rivers, and lagoons, it is overlooked by the vacationing public. The campground is quite large by state park standards and has lots of facilities. This one is quiet and undisturbed.

FACILITIES: Here you can enjoy coastal camping at its best on one of 100 sites, all with water and electric hookups, picnic tables, and grills. The bathhouse is modern, kept scrupulously clean, is handicapped accessible, and has flush toilets and hot showers. There are also facilities for youth and group camping.

RULES AND REGULATIONS: No pets, but guide dogs are welcome. Quiet time 10 PM until 8 AM.

SECURITY: Very good. The gates are locked from sunset to 8 AM. Round-the-clock security by a resident park manager. Campers are provided with the combination to the gate lock.

NEAREST SERVICES: Three miles away in Ormond Beach.

RECREATION: There's a boat ramp and dock, a nature trail, a park museum where you can buy real Florida gifts, food and drink, and rent canoes. Most of the park's recreation facilities are handicapped accessible, especially the paved trail to the dock. Picnicking, canoeing the lagoons, rivers, and creeks; hiking the nature trail; nature study, bird watching, and wildlife photography; fishing for striped bass, speckled trout, bluefish, redfish, flounder, mullet, sheephead, and whiting.

OPEN: Year round.

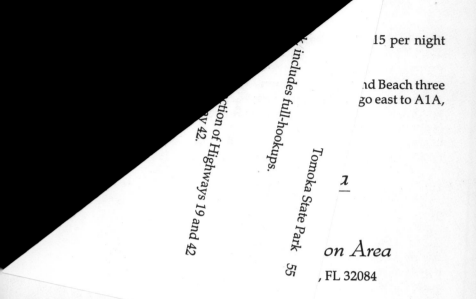

15 per night

...d Beach three
...go east to A1A,

Tomoka State Park
55

ction of Highways 19 and 42.

...y 42.

...k includes full-hookups.

a

on Area

, FL 32084

The Spanish settled St. Aug... ...making it the first permanent city to be established in Americ... This is where you'll find Anastasia State Recreation Area. The Spaniards, in search of materials, crossed the Matanzas River and established quarries for "coquina," a durable material ideal for their purposes. The same rock was used to build the nearby Castillo de San Marcos, the nation's oldest masonry fortress. Today, those same quarries are a part of the Anastasia State Recreation Area. This is the region where Juan Ponce de Leon landed. He was smitten with the abundance of plant life and wildflowers. "Florida" was the name given to the land that was claimed for Spain.

A variety of shorebirds, such as gulls, terns, sandpipers, pelicans, egrets, and herons inhabit the park. During spring and fall, many migratory birds visit the marshes and wooded areas on their journeys to and from their natural habitats in Northern United States.

FACILITIES: Coastal camping on modern, full-service campsites complete with water and electric hookups, handicapped accessible restrooms, hot showers, picnic tables, and grills. There are also a variety of concessions. Rent sailboards and take lessons on Salt Run. Bicycles, umbrellas, paddle cruisers, and beach chairs all can be rented on the beach.

RULES & REGULATIONS: No pets, but guide dogs are welcome. Alcohol and firearms prohibited. Quiet time 10 PM until 8 PM.

SECURITY: Very good. Round-the-clock by a resident park manager. The gates are locked from sunset to 8 AM. Campers are provided with the combination to the gate lock, allowing free exit and access after the park has closed.

RECREATION: Bird watching, fishing in the surf or the lagoon (sea trout, bluefish, pompano, whiting, redfish, and flounder),canoeing, hiking along the Atlantic beaches, and picnicking (there are three separate areas located along the main drive).

NEAREST SERVICES: There's a concession shop on the property where you can purchase light snacks and small supplies. Other than that, there are nearby grocery stores, hardware stores where you can purchase LP gas, fast food restaurants and a variety of retail shops on St. Augustine Beach.

RATES: $15 per night from October 1 through February 28; $17 per night March 1 through September 30.

OPEN: Year round.

HOW TO GET THERE: Take A1A south from St. Augustine to Route 3. The Recreation Area is located at St. Augustine Beach.

Bryn Mawr Ocean Resort

4850 A1A S., St. Augustine, FL 32084
(904) 471-3353

This is the only RV park on St. Augustine Beach. It is a commercial campground with more than 140 fully landscaped, paved sites right on the beach, only five miles from downtown St. Augustine. The camp is very busy and crowded in the high season, which can be a bit of a problem, but it's convenient, with plenty to see and do.

FACILITIES: Accepts full hookup units only. Rental units are available. The restrooms are clean and well-maintained with hot showers. All sites have cable TV and telephone hookups. The laundry room is equipped with modern machines and it, too, is clean and well-maintained. Sewage disposal is available.

RULES & REGULATIONS: No tents. No motorcycles. Reservations recommended for the period March 1 through September 30. Pets are allowed if kept on a leash.

SECURITY: Excellent. Round-the-clock security. Traffic control at the gate. Security guard on duty after 7 PM. Regular patrols through the night. Security during the day by on-site staff.

NEAREST SERVICES: On the property. There's a full-service store where you'll find almost all of what you need, including groceries, paper goods, ice, RV supplies, LP gas refills by weight or meter. The campground is just one mile from the nearest grocery store. There are several nice restaurants only yards away and lining the beach.

RECREATION: There's a large swimming pool, lighted tennis, shuffleboard, volleyball and basketball courts. Playground, picnic shelters, tables and grills are also provided. The staff offers a variety of concessions, including rental bicycles, paddle boats, umbrellas and beach chairs. A program of planned group activities is organized by a resident recreation director during the winter months. This includes organized local tours and sightseeing. If you like to do things on your own, there are plenty of tour operators just a phone call away. Other activities you might enjoy are bird watching, fishing in the surf for sea trout, bluefish, pompano, whiting, redfish and flounder, deep sea charter fishing out of St. Augustine, canoeing, sailing, hiking along the Atlantic beaches, and picnicking.

ATTRACTIONS: St. Augustine Alligator Farm, St. Augustine Spanish Quarter, Castillo de San Marcos, Lighthouse Museum of St. Augustine, Fernandina Harbor Marina, and the Palace Saloon at Fernandina Beach are nearby. Jacksonville is just up the road to the north where you can visit the Zoo and the Riverwalk, Marineland of Florida is just to the south, and the Morningside Nature Center is to the west in Gainesville. You might also like to visit Guana River State Park, Crescent Beach, the pari-mutuel dog track at Orange Park, Flagler Beach, and the Fort Matanzas National Monument. Be sure to take a walking tour of the Historic District in St. Augustine and the Castillo de San Marcos.

RATES: Sites closest to the ocean are $34 per night for two persons; those in the next rank $30; and the sites farthest from the ocean are $26 per night.

OPEN: Year round.

HOW TO GET THERE: From the junction of I-95 and Highway 206, go seven miles east on Highway 206, then three miles north on US A1A.

Faver-Dykes State Park

1000 Faver-Dykes Road, St. Augustine, FL 32086
(904) 794-0997

Faver-Dykes is a full-service state park with plenty to see and do for the entire family. The 750-acre park incorporates pine and hardwood forests, hammocks, pinelands, bayheads, swamps, and marshes. The wild environment presents an illusion of remoteness, reminiscent of the landscape as it must have been when the Spanish explorers landed on Florida's shores in the late 1560s.

The diverse plant life provides habitats for an abundance of wildlife, including many species of wading birds, waterfowl, alligators, and otters. Deer, turkeys, hawks, owls, squirrels, bobcats, foxes, and opossums make their homes in the uplands close to Pellicer Creek and are often seen along the creek itself.

The campground is small and often booked months in advance, but, due to its size, is never crowded.

FACILITIES: The park has 30 modern campsites complete with water and electric hookups, picnic tables and grills. The restrooms have flush toilets, the bathhouse hot showers, and they are handicapped accessible. Youth camping facilities are available to non-profit groups.

SECURITY: Very good. Round-the-clock security by a resident park manager. The gates are locked from sunset to 8 AM. Campers are provided with the combination to the gate lock.

NEAREST SERVICES: There are several fast food restaurants and gas stations at the junction of I-95 and US 1, but the nearest full-service facilities are at Palm Coast, some eight miles to the south on I-95, or Crescent Beach about the same distance away on A1A. Both cities have grocery stores, hardware stores where you can purchase LP gas, and fast food restaurants. Fine dining is available, along with a variety of retail shops and malls in St. Augustine 15 miles to the north.

RECREATION: There are two loop hiking trails. One begins near the picnic area and winds through the pinelands, the other begins at the camping area and takes hikers through a mature hardwood hammock. A boat ramp gives access to Pellicer Creek, and a picnic area overlooks the creek. Activities include: bird watching, wildlife photography, boating, fishing in Pellicer Creek (speckled trout, redfish, sheephead, and flounder), canoeing, picnicking, and hiking.

NEARBY ATTRACTIONS: Bulow Creek State Park is in Ormond Beach just to the south; the Bulow Plantation Ruins State Historic Site is three miles west of Flagler Beach; Ormond Beach itself is about 17 miles south of the park; Daytona Beach and the International Speedway are just to the south of Ormond Beach. Marineland of Florida is less than two miles away on A1A, the Gamble Rogers Memorial State Recreation Area is at Flagler Beach on A1A, and the Fort Matanzas National Monument is less than five miles to the north, also on A1A. Historic St. Augustine and Castillo de San Marcos are 15 miles north via Highway A1A or Interstate 95, and Jacksonville is 29 miles farther north beyond St. Augustine.

RATES: $8 per night.

OPEN: Year round.

HOW TO GET THERE: The park is 15 miles south of St. Augustine at the intersection of I-95 and US Highway 1.

Marineland Camping Resort

9741 Ocean Shore Blvd., St. Augustine, FL 32086-8618
(904) 471-4700

This is a top-of-the-line oceanside camping resort adjacent to and operated by Marineland of Florida. The facility is in a fairly remote area on the Atlantic beaches, surrounded by pine flatwoods and hardwood hammocks, bayheads, swamps, and marshes. It's very busy most of the year. Stay away if you don't like crowds.

FACILITIES: There are 110 sites, all with full-service hookups to 30 amps, telephone and cable TV hookups; 40 are pull-throughs. Rental tents available. The bathhouses are clean, modern, have flush toilets and hot showers, and are all handicapped accessible.

Sewage disposal is available to overnig
room is clean and well-maintained, and
handy to the sites.

RULES & REGULATIONS: One pet per site. Quie
until 7 AM.

SECURITY: Excellent. The campground is kept under surveill
around the clock by Marineland security staff. Regular patro
through the night.

NEAREST SERVICES: There's a full-service store on the property
where you can buy most of the basics, including bread, milk and
canned goods, but the nearest grocery store is a Publix supermarket
almost 11 miles away to the north. Be sure to stock up before you
arrive. There are three restaurants nearby, including the Dolphin at
Marineland. RV supplies, including LP, gas are available on the
property by weight and meter, as well as gasoline, marine gasoline
and ice.

RECREATION: The campground has a large recreation hall and a
pavilion with coin-operated games. There's a nice heated swimming pool and a wading pool for the kids with lots of room to relax
in the sunshin . There's also a boat ramp and dock, sports fields,
two tennis courts, a basketball court, and several hiking trails.
Activities include: bird watching, wildlife photography, boating,
fishing the surf or nearby saltwater creeks for sea trout, bluefish,
pompano, whiting, sheephead, redfish and flounder. Other popular pastimes include hiking along the Atlantic beaches, canoeing,
and picnicking. Planned group activities are organized during the
winter months.

NEARBY ATTRACTIONS: Daytona Beach and the International
Speedway are about 30 miles away, just to the south of Ormond
Beach on Highway A1A. The Gamble Rogers Memorial State Rec-
reation Area is at Flagler Beach, also on A1A, and the Fort Matanzas
National Monument is less than five miles to the north. Ormond
Beach is about 25 miles south of the park via Highway A1A; Bulow
Creek State Park is in Ormond Beach just to the south of Flagler
Beach – 15 miles south; the Bulow Plantation Ruins State Historic
Site is three miles west of Flagler Beach; Historic St. Augustine is 17
miles north via Highway A1A or Interstate 95, and Jacksonville is
29 miles farther north beyond St. Augustine.

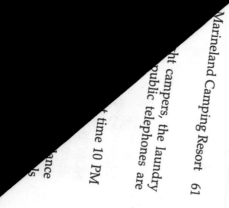

up to five persons; includes

...ground is adjacent to the Ma-
...n of St. Augustine on Highway
...Highway 206, go two miles east
...iles south on Highway A1A.

Camp Resort

4125 Coastal Highway, ... Augustine, FL 32095-1418
(904) 824-1806

This is another coastal campground. Set on more than 60 acres of private property on the Intracoastal Waterway, it is in an area heavily wooded with pine flatwoods and hardwood hammocks, bayheads, swamps, and marshes. There are more than 500 feet of Atlantic ocean frontage with a wide sandy beach. There's also a river that bounds the property. It can be busy at times, but never too crowded, and the staff is friendly and helpful.

FACILITIES: Of the 120 private, shady sites, 85 have full-service hookups, cable TV and telephone. There are only 18 pull-throughs, so you'll need to book early if you need this type of site. The bathhouses are very clean with lots of hot water for the showers; the facilities are all handicapped accessible. The laundry room is also clean and well maintained. Sewage disposal is offered to overnight campers, and rental tents are available.

RULES & REGULATIONS: Pets welcome if kept quiet and on a leash. Tents are welcome. Quiet time is 10 PM until 7 AM.

SECURITY: Very good. Gated with security handled by resident staff.

NEAREST SERVICES: There's a full-service store on the property where you can purchase the basics: bread, milk, etc. (no meat), paper goods, RV supplies, LP gas by weight, and ice. The nearest grocery store is five miles away in St. Augustine. There are two full-service restaurants on the property: one on the riverbank, the other on the ocean. Bait and tackle is available at the store. There are no beach chairs or umbrellas, so bring your own.

RECREATION: Group activities in the large recreation hall, including movies, volleyball, shuffleboard, horseshoes and indoor games. You can go swimming either in the ocean or the swimming pool, and boating and windsurfing are possibilities – there's a boat ramp and dock. If you like to fish, you can do it from the dock or beach. You can also enjoy sunning on the beach or riverbank and hiking along the beach.

NEARBY ATTRACTIONS: Historic St. Augustine is just five miles away. There you can visit the Alligator Farm, St. Augustine Spanish Quarter, Castillo de San Marcos, Lighthouse Museum of St. Augustine, and lots more. Jacksonville, 30 miles to the north of St. Augustine, is where you'll find the Riverwalk and Zoo. Marineland of Florida is 17 miles south on A1A; the Morningside Nature Center is to the west in Gainesville; there's a pari-mutuel dog track at Orange Park. Flagler Beach is 30 miles to the south, beyond the Fort Matanzas National Monument.

RATES: $24 per night for full hookups.

OPEN: All year.

HOW TO GET THERE: From the junction of I-95 and Highway 208, go east to US Highway 1, then south on Highway 1 to the junction of Highway A1A, then four miles on A1A.

The Panhandle

Florida's northwest is still very much overlooked by the vacationing public. It's slowly but surely being discovered, but there's still a long way to go. The area encompasses some of the state's best beaches, attractions and parks, almost all of them still unspoiled. Some areas are quite remote, windswept, and isolated; some are more accessible, very much a part of the modern metropolitan experience. From Pensacola in the west, all the way to Cedar Key on the Upper Gulf Coast, there's much to see and do. It's a land of crystal rivers, rolling hills, snow-white beaches and sea oats, moss-draped trees, and fine old homes on avenues lined with tropical trees and shrubs. It's the legendary Suwannee River and remote barrier islands where only the soft sounds of the surf and the lonely call of a wheeling seagull disturb the silence. Here are a dozen or more state and national parks are located. These are dedicated to the preservation of all that Florida once was: its endangered wildlife, plants, and environment.

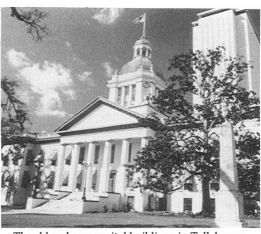

The old and new capital buildings in Tallahassee.

This is not a land of glitz and high times. True, you can find some of that if you look hard enough for it, but it's a place to spend quiet hours on the beach, hiking beautiful nature trails, bird watching, and fishing. It's a place to get away from the noise and brass of the resorts of the south.

It's a historical place: Pensacola is the second oldest city in the nation, if not the oldest, as it claims to be. And evidence of its long and turbulent history can be found in the Pensacola Historic Museum and in three lovingly restored preservation areas: North Hill, Palofax, and Seville Historic Districts.

From Pensacola, the Emerald Coast, named for the sparkling green waters of the Gulf of Mexico, stretches eastward through the tiny seaside towns of Fort Walton Beach, Destin, South Walton and on to Panama City Beach, where you'll find life much closer to that of Florida's more famous resorts. Next is the St. Joseph Peninsula, Apalachicola, and the shore of the Upper Gulf Coast.

Pensacola is northwest Florida's second city. This community, famous for its miles of sugar-white sand, also offers a wide range of activities and attractions: beaches, museums, restaurants, shops, and nightclubs, a nationally renowned aviation museum, and a zoo that features more than 700 animals. It's a delightful mixture of past and present. The flags of five nations have flown over the city, and its fondly restored downtown historic district displays a past that stretches back more than 400 years. Nowhere is it displayed better than the sites in and around Historic Pensacola Village.

If you're a fisherman, you'll probably find no better place to angle than Pensacola. Each year, the city sponsors a number of nationally and internationally known tournaments, including the International Billfish Tournament in July. Charters are available the year-round.

Gulf Islands National Seashore is a long chain of barrier islands that follow the coastline from South Mississippi to West Florida. It protects and preserves the unspoiled beaches, wide open spaces and historic sites from the wind and surf. At the heart of the National Seashore, Pensacola is flanked by a pair of barrier islands: Perdido Key to the west and Santa Rosa Island, better known as Pensacola Beach, to the east. These two islands offer miles of white sand, crystal green waters, beautiful vistas, and plenty of peace and quiet.

Fort Walton Beach and Destin, just to the east of Pensacola, represent the heart of the Emerald Coast. The area's beaches, more than 24 miles of them, are consistently rated among the best in the world. Surrounded by the Gulf, Choctawhatchee Bay, Santa Rosa Sound, innumerable lakes and bayous, and scattered throughout with sand pines and blossoming magnolias, this stretch of the Panhandle coast comes as close to paradise as you can imagine. With an average of 343 sunny days per year, you're practically guaranteed the very best weather.

From Fort Walton Beach to Destin, more than 100 restaurants serve the "freshest seafood in Florida." These range from casual beach and bay-side seafood shacks to gracious ante-bellum estates and elegant cafés. The local operators claim there's always at least 20 types of fish available.

Fort Walton Beach is a typical little seaside town with all the usual attractions: beaches, walks, aquarium, fairgrounds, gift shops, watersports and restaurants. Destin, known as the "World's Luckiest Fishing Village," is the deep-sea fishing capital of northern Florida. This area of the Gulf yields more billfish each year than any other, and the little town boasts five saltwater world records. On the waterfront, dozens of experienced charter captains are available to take you in the search for "the big one."

Panama City Beach is the Panhandle's resort area. More than 27 miles of beaches unroll in a breathtaking display of natural beauty. And, believe it or not, this is where you'll find the nation's best beach. Rated the "Number One Beach" in America for 1995 by Dr. Stephen Leatherman, coastal geologist at the University of Maryland, the St. Andrews State Recreation Area still remains virtually undiscovered by the vacationing public.

Like many other coastal resorts, Panama City claims to be the "Seafood Capital of the World." Is the claim a good one? You'll have to judge for yourself. What you will find is a diversity of fine and colorful restaurants serving everything from fresh amberjack to oysters, and from lobster to shark. Beyond its restaurants and cafés, beaches and shops, you'll find there's plenty to see and do: golf, zoo, amusement parks, museums, and dancing the until the wee hours at any one of the 50 night clubs and bars.

Tallahassee, the state capital, is a city of opportunity. It's an intimate city, old-world, nestled in the first foothills of the Appalachian Mountains where the rolling hills are dotted with plantations, towering pines, cypress, dogwoods, magnolias and hundreds of shimmering lakes, springs, rivers, and swamps. It's a town where present meets past among the historic downtown districts, along the canopied roads, where live oaks draped with Spanish moss line the walkways and parks. Here, historic buildings that have lived through centuries of national development co-exist with the modern structures of state government. [Insert photo] This is Florida's plantation country: more than 70 of them are scattered among the fields, forests, springs, and rivers between Tallahassee and Thomasville, Georgia. America's most famous "Tarzan," (Johnny Weissmuller and Maureen O'Sullivan) filmed many of the water scenes here. Tallahassee itself lists 122 properties on the National Register of Historic Places.

The seafood lover is in for a treat in Tallahassee. With the Gulf and more than a dozen fishing villages less than 40 miles away, it's no wonder the dining is excellent. Of all the good food there is to offer, two delicacies are worth a mention here: Apalachicola oysters and Panacea blue crabs. Chefs worldwide demand the famous oyster, and Panacea is, without doubt, the "Blue Crab Capital of the World." You can enjoy both at any one of a hundred fine restaurants throughout the Tallahassee area.

The shopping, too, is an experience to remember. From the vast shopping malls to the tiny, out-of-the-way arcade, you'll enjoy the thrill of the hunt for unusual gifts.

Apalachicola

St. George Island State Park

Box 62, Eastpoint, FL 32328
(904) 927-2111

St. George is another of Florida's Gulf Coast barrier islands, and probably one of the best recreational locations that park system has to offer. Set to the east of the St. Joseph Peninsula, St. Vincent National Wildlife Refuge, and across the bay to the southeast of Apalachicola, St. George Island is one Florida's premier nature centers. The sometimes wild, desolate environment offers the local bird and marine life the best of habitats. Nine miles of sandy shoreline and grassy flats provide nesting grounds for plovers, willets, terns, black skimmers, and many other shore birds.

FACILITIES: There are full-service campsites with water and electric hookups; a bathhouse with flush toilets and hot showers, all handicapped accessible; and a laundry room. Youth and primitive camping is also available.

RULES & REGULATIONS: No pets, but guide dogs are welcome. Alcohol and firearms prohibited. Do not feed wild animals.

SECURITY: Very good. Round-the-clock security by a resident park manager. The gates are locked from sunset to 8 AM. Campers are provided with the combination to the gate lock, allowing free exit and access after the park has closed.

NEAREST SERVICES: The nearest full-service supermarket is about 16 miles away on the mainland in Eastpoint. It would be wise to stock up before you arrive on the island.

RECREATION: There's a swimming area, several nature trails, a boat ramp, showers for public use, and a picnic area. Once again, the outdoor living and activities are the focus here. The surf fishing is claimed to be the best on the Gulf Coast; then there's swimming and snorkeling, hiking along miles of sandy beaches, sunbathing, nature study, bird watching, and boating.

NEARBY ATTRACTIONS: Florida's state capital, Tallahassee, with all of its sights and attractions, is about 50 miles north along Highway 369. St. Joseph Peninsula State Recreation Area is just a few miles west beyond Apalachicola on Highway 98; the Constitution Convention State Museum is in Port St. Joe, also along Highway 98; and Natural Bridge Battlefield State Historic Site is six miles east of Woodville and 12 miles southeast of Tallahassee off Highway 363. Wakulla Springs State Recreation Area and Lodge is just 14 miles south on Highway 267. If you like a little action, there's a pari-mutuel dog track near Monticello on Highway 57/19. The Apalachicola National Forest stretches to the north of Apalachicola. The city and beaches of Apalachicola itself are just across the water on Highway 319/98; and the John Gorrie State Museum is on Sixth Street in Apalachicola. Ochlockonee River State Park is just to the northeast on Highway 98, Alligator Point is even closer to the northeast and the historic little town of St. Marks is about 20 miles to the east. Panacea, "Blue Crab Capital of the World," is just to the northeast on Highway 98. You'll find many more attractions listed along with the other campgrounds in the region.

RATES: $8 per night

OPEN: Year round.

HOW TO GET THERE: The Park is 10 miles southeast of Eastpoint on St. George Island. From Apalachicola, drive east across the John Gorrie Memorial Bridge to the junction of Highways 30 and 65. Turn right onto 65 and proceed to Highway G1A. Turn onto G1A and drive across Apalachicola Bay to St. George Island. There you'll turn left and drive on to the park.

Bristol

Torreya State Park

Route 2, Box 70, Bristol, FL 32321
(904) 643-2674

The rare torreya tree (from which the park gets its name), the extraordinary high bluffs along the Apalachicola River, and the deep ravines carved into the rocks by thousands of years of water erosion, make the area around Torreya State Park a very special place. Sometimes rising to more than 150 feet, the densely forested bluffs provide a natural refuge for many rare and beautiful species of wildlife. The torreya tree, once plentiful throughout the area, was almost destroyed by disease. It is now found only on the high bluffs along the Apalachicola River. There are other rare trees and plants here too, including the Florida yew tree and the US Champion winged elm, and a great variety of wild shrubs and flowers. And, although the campground may be somewhat limited in size, you'll appreciate the immaculate facilities provided by what is claimed to be one of Florida's "most peaceful and scenic parks."

FACILITIES: There are 35 sites, of which 16 have water and electric hookups; all have tables. The bathhouse has flush toilets and hot showers; facilities are handicapped accessible. For campers who like to rough it, there are two primitive campsites, a youth camp-site, and a picnic area with covered shelters.

RULES & REGULATIONS: No pets, but guide dogs are welcome. Alcohol and firearms prohibited. Do not feed wild animals.

SECURITY: Very good. Round-the-clock security by a resident park manager. The gates are locked from sunset to 8 AM. Campers are provided with the combination to the gate lock, allowing free exit and access after the park has closed.

NEAREST SERVICES: In Bristol about five miles to the south on Highway 270.

RECREATION: Hikers and backpackers will enjoy the seven-mile-long Loop Trail, the Apalachicola Bluffs Trail and the National Recreational Trail, while others will find the Weeping Ridge Trail a pleasant, less strenuous walk. For nature lovers, Torraya has more than 100 species of wild birds, and almost as many animals.

NEARBY ATTRACTIONS: Florida Caverns State Park is just to the northwest, about 20 miles, near Marianna. Three Rivers State Recreation Area is on the shores of Lake Seminole about 12 miles north on Highway 271, Falling Waters State Recreation Area is about 50 miles to the west along Interstate 10, Ponce de Leon Springs State Recreation Area is even farther west along Interstate 10, Dead Lakes State Recreation Area is some 35 miles to the south near Wewahitchka on Highway 71. There's a pari-mutuel dog track at Ebro about 55 miles southwest on Highway 79, Big Bend Jai-Alai pari-mutuel about 10 miles southeast off Interstate 10 on Highway 270A south. You'll find many more attractions listed along with the other campgrounds in the region.

RATES: $8 per night.

OPEN: Year round.

HOW TO GET THERE: The park is on Highway 12, 13 miles north of Bristol, and about eight miles south of I-10.

Chipley

Falling Waters State Recreation Area

Route 5, Box 660, Chipley, FL 32428
(901) 638-6130

The main feature of the park is something of an anomaly. The 67-foot waterfall from which the area takes its name is natural enough, but the Falling Waters Sink is something different. The Sink is a 100-foot-deep, 20-foot-wide cylindrical pit into which a small stream flows. Once in the pit, the water simply disappears. It's quite a mystery. The campground and park are small but quite isolated. The small number of sites makes for a companionable atmosphere.

FACILITIES: There are 24 sites, all equipped with water, electric hookups, picnic tables, and grills. The restrooms are handicapped accessible, and there are flush toilets and hot showers. There's also a youth camping facility for use by organized, non-profit groups.

RULES & REGULATIONS: No pets, but guide dogs are welcome. Alcohol and firearms prohibited. Do not feed wild animals.

SECURITY: Very good. Round-the-clock security by a resident park manager. The gates are locked from sunset to 8 AM. Campers are provided with the combination to the gate lock, allowing free exit and access after the park has closed.

NEAREST SERVICES: About two miles away in Chipley.

RECREATION: There's a swimming area at the Sink, a campfire circle, several nature trails, and a picnic area with a playground for the kids close by. You can also go hiking, picnicking, canoeing, and bird and nature watching. Woodpeckers, bobwhite, quail, red foxes, and fox squirrels may be seen. The fishing in the lake is good, and more fishing is available at Blue Lake, about a ½ mile to the west on Highway 77, where you'll find a public-access boat ramp. If you like to play golf, Falling Waters Country Club is right next door on Highway 77A.

NEARBY ATTRACTIONS: Florida Caverns State Recreation Area is just to the north of Marianna, which is about 10 miles east along Interstate 10, Ponce de Leon Springs State Recreation Area is about 22 miles west along Interstate 10, Panama City and the beaches are about 40 miles south on Highway 77, Tallahassee is some 70 miles west along Interstate 10, and there's a pari-mutuel dog track at Ebro, about 30 miles southwest on Highway 79. You'll find more attractions listed along with the other campgrounds in this section.

RATES: $8 per night. Reservations are not accepted. As small as the campground is, however, you'd better call ahead and make sure there's a site available.

OPEN: Year round.

HOW TO GET THERE: Falling Waters State Recreation Area is three miles south of Chipley, off SR 77A. From the junction of Interstate 10 and Highway 77, drive south on 77 for about ¾ mile, then turn right onto 77A and drive about a mile to the park.

Dead Lakes

Dead Lakes Recreation Area

PO Box 989, Wewahitchka, FL 32465
(904) 639-2702

Dead Lakes is one of those untamed places where one goes to get close to nature. The area is said to have been formed when great sand bars, thrown up by the current of the Apalachicola River, blocked the Chipola River. The waters of the Chipola rose, creating a vast floodplain and killing thousands of trees – thus the areas name.

Today, the park is a naturalist's dream. Longleaf pines, sweetbay, magnolia and cypress abound. The animal population includes the fox, the cotton rat, raccoon, opossum, deer, rabbit, skunk, beaver, turtle, alligator, and a variety of snakes. The campground is a fairly small one, but what it lacks in size it makes up for in aesthetics and recreational opportunities. Dead Lakes is a nationally famous fishing spot.

FACILITIES: There are 29 campsites with water and electric hookups; the restrooms are handicapped accessible. The bathhouse has flush toilets and hot showers. The campsites have tables and grills.

RULES & REGULATIONS: No pets, but guide dogs are welcome. Alcohol and firearms prohibited. Do not feed wild animals.

SECURITY: Very good. Round-the-clock security by a resident park manager. The gates are locked from sunset to 8 AM. Campers are provided with the combination to the gate lock, allowing free exit and access after the park has closed.

NEAREST SERVICES: About a mile away in Wewahitchka.

RECREATION: Several thousand acres of deep, still waters, forests and wetlands provide numerous opportunities for boating, canoeing, swimming, hiking, bird watching, and photography. Fishing in the lake is said to be excellent (largemouth, smallmouth and striped bass, speckled perch, bream, bluegill, catfish, and shellcracker). There's a public-access boat ramp in the park, and at least a dozen more scattered along the shores of the lake.

NEARBY ATTRACTIONS: To the south, via Highways 71 and 98, lie St. Joseph's Bay, Apalachicola, and St. George Island; to the west, via Highway 22, Panama City; to the northwest, via Highways 71 and 20, Tallahassee. St. Joseph Peninsula State Recreation Area is just a few miles west on Highway 98. The Constitution Convention State Museum is in Port St. Joe, also along Highway 98. Natural Bridge Battlefield State Historic Site is six miles east of Woodville and 12 miles southeast of Tallahassee off Highway 363. Wakulla Springs State Recreation Area and Lodge is just 14 miles south on Highway 267. You can visit the pari-mutuel dog track near Monticello on Highway 57/19. The Apalachicola National Forest stretches east of the lake and north of Apalachicola. The beaches in and around Apalachicola are within easy reach on Highways 98; and the John Gorrie State Museum is on Sixth Street in Apalachicola. Alligator Point and Ochlockonee River State Park are about 55 miles to the east via Highway 22. The historic little town of St. Marks is about 20 miles further to the east. Panacea, "Blue Crab Capital of the World," is just to the north of Alligator Point on Highway 98. There are more attractions listed along with the other campgrounds in this section.

RATES: $8 per night.

OPEN: Year round.

HOW TO GET THERE: The park is one mile north of Wewa-hitchka of SR 71.

Destin

This quaint little town on the Emerald Coast has only recently been discovered by the vacationing public. For many years it was just a stop off along the way to somewhere better. But then people began to notice the miles of white sandy beaches, the clear green water of the ocean, and the quiet, lonely vistas. They found the fishing boats, wharves and tiny restaurants, and they began to stay. Over the last few years, tourism has exploded. Developers soon followed the tourists and hotels began to spring up everywhere. In no time, the coast road through the small fishing village and beyond was lined with amusements: mini-golf, water slides, gift shops, rollercoasters, bars. Today, Destin is a self-contained resort where you can find plenty of nightlife and action. The beaches are just as pristine and attractive as they were before the arrival of the developer: great white dunes and stands of waving seagrass that stretch into the distance as far as the eye can see. And they are never very busy, even at the height of the season. Offshore, the dolphins play in the surf, pelicans and a variety of seabirds dive and pester the sun-worshipers on the beach. In the evening, the sunsets are spectacular.

Emerald Coast RV Resort

Route 1, Box 2820, Santa Rosa Beach, FL 32458
(800) 232-2478

Conveniently located five minutes from one of the nation's top 10 beaches, this campground offers an extensive range of facilities and recreational opportunities. It's one of only four campgrounds in Florida to receive a 10/10/10 rating from *Trailer Life*. By Florida campground standards, it's not a large one. Very upscale, the emphasis is on comfort more than roughing it. The sites are large, 60 x 80 feet, and everything has been designed to facilitate easy living.

FACILITIES: Of the 100 available sites, all have full-service hookups to 50 amps, cable TV and telephone hookups. They can accommodate even the largest of RVs. The roads are all paved, there's a spacious, well-equipped laundry room, and and a luxurious, tiled bathhouse. There are patios, tables and grills on every site.

RULES & REGULATIONS: Pets are welcome if kept under control, but tents and pop-up trailers are not permitted.

SECURITY: Excellent. The campground is gated and there's a guard on duty around the clock.

NEAREST SERVICES: There's a full-service store on-site and LP gas is available by weight or meter.

RECREATION: Lots to do here – one of the best beaches in North America is just five minutes away, there's an on-site nature trail, a large, heated swimming pool, a well-equipped recreation hall, an 18-foot deep lake where you can fish (catfish, bluegill, striped bass, and the Georgia hybrid giant bream). If you would like to go deep-sea fishing, the staff will arrange a charter; if not, you can cast your line out from the beach. The campground has its own tennis courts, and all the usual court games are available, too. A shuttle is provided free of charge to take you to the beaches and the shops. There's also a recreation director on hand to organize group activities and day trips.

NEARBY ATTRACTIONS: Like Destin to the north, so it is here at Santa Rosa Beach. Other than the endless miles of beaches and dunes, there's not much sightseeing to do in the immediate vicinity of the campground. You might, however, visit Fort Walton Beach, where you'll find plenty of shops and bars, Panama City is about 50 miles south, Ponce De Leon Springs State Recreation Area is just a few miles to the north, and the huge Santa Rosa Shopping Mall is on the western side of Fort Walton Beach. If you don't mind driving, you can visit The Museum of Man in the Sea at Panama City, where you can see all sorts of interesting exhibits related to man's attempt to live and operate under the sea. Shipwreck Island Water Park is also in Panama City, Apalachicola is not far away. The Fort Gadsden State Historic Site is at Marianna; Dead Lakes State Recreation Area is at Wewahitchka; and the St. Joseph's Peninsula State Park is on the peninsula at St. Joseph's Bay.

RATES: Rates start at around $22 per night for two persons; weekly and monthly rates are available on request.

OPEN: Year round.

HOW TO GET THERE: From Destin, drive eight miles south on Highway 98, then .3 miles south on Highway 30A.

Grayton Beach State Recreation Area

Route 2, Box 6600, Santa Rosa Beach, FL 32459
(904) 231-4210

Grayton Beach is one of the oldest cities on Florida's Gulf Coast, and the 356-acre recreation area offers its visitors plenty to see and do. The beaches are white, soft, and wonderful (Grayton Beach is also on the list of "America's Best Beaches") and the sea is clear and warm. The campground is small, but you'll find it well-managed, and a great place to enjoy the sea, sun, and sand.

FACILITIES: There are 37 campsites, all with water and electric hookups, picnic tables and grills. The bathhouse has flush toilets, hot showers and plenty of hot water. The restrooms are handicapped accessible.

RULES & REGULATIONS: No pets, but guide dogs are welcome. Alcohol and firearms prohibited. Do not feed wild animals.

SECURITY: Very good. Round-the-clock security by a resident park manager. The gates are locked from sunset to 8 AM. Campers are provided with the combination to the gate lock, allowing free exit and access after the park has closed.

NEAREST SERVICES: About 4½ miles away in Sandestin. Be sure to stock up before you arrive. The

The boardwalk at Grayton Beach.

shops, restaurants and bars in Destin itself are about 10 miles away; Fort Walton Beach and the malls are about 20 miles away.

RECREATION: This campground and recreation area is right on the beach, and what a beach it is. As far as the eye can see, the sugar-white strip of sand stretches to the east and west. Surf fishing, wind surfing, and jet skiing are popular pastimes. You can rent jet skis and windsurfers a few miles to the east on the shores of Choctawhatchee Bay. Swimming and sunbathing on the ever-quiet beach are lazy, day-long experiences; take a book and spend a day or two. If you like to hike, there are several trails inside the 356-acre park. You can go for miles in either direction along the water's edge. The fishing is good in either the ocean or the lake on the property.

NEARBY ATTRACTIONS: Destin and its fast-paced Miracle Strip is just a few miles to the west. Fort Walton Beach, where you'll find plenty of shops, restaurants, bars and clubs, is a few miles farther on beyond Okaloosa Island, where you'll also find lots to see and do. Panama City is about 50 miles to the south. There you can visit The Museum of Man in the Sea and Shipwreck Island Water Park. For a long day out, you might like to drive past Panama City to St.Joseph's Peninsula and Apalachicola.

RATES: October through February, $8 per night. March through September, $14 per night. If you just want to visit and use the beachfront facilities (parking, restrooms, etc.). Up to 8 people can stay all day for $3.50. The park can be quite busy for camping, so call ahead.

OPEN: Year round.

HOW TO GET THERE: From Destin, drive east on Highway 98/30 to its junction with Highway 30A. Turn right onto 30A. This will lead you to the park. OR continue east on Highway 98 to its junction with Highway 283, which will lead directly to the park.

Holiday Travel Park

5380 Highway 98E, Destin, FL 32541-4114
(904) 837-6334

This campgroung is on the beach, with shady oceanside sites, and all the fun, sea, sand, fishing you can handle.

FACILITIES: Of the 257 sites, 137 have full-service hook-ups, and 18 are pull-throughs. The bathhouses are roomy and tiled with plenty of hot water. You'll find all of the standard facilities: sewage disposal, laundry, picnic tables, etc.

RULES & REGULATIONS: Pets are welcome, but must be kept under control at all times. Quiet time is 10 PM to 7 AM.

SECURITY: Good. Handled by live-in staff.

NEAREST SERVICES: There's a full-service store on-site where you can purchase most of the essentials. Shops and supermarkets are a few miles away in Destin. On the property there is a gift shop, gasoline pumps, and you can purchase LP gas by weight or meter.

RECREATION: There's a huge recreation building, a large swimming pool with an even bigger patio, and a variety of court games. The focus of entertainment, however, is on the beaches and the ocean. The sand and surf are only a few feet from your site, and the charter fishing fleet in Destin is less than 10 minutes away. The fishing is excellent, both from the beaches and on the ocean, and the boats never have to go too far from shore to find the action: marlin, sailfish, tuna, and more. If you like to hike, you'll find no place better to do it than the many miles of firm sandy beach. For tennis and golf enthusiasts, there's all sorts of opportunities close by in Destin and a little farther to the north in Fort Walton Beach.

NEARBY ATTRACTIONS: Other than its many beach areas and resorts there's not much in the way of conventional sightseeing here. You might like to visit Fort Walton Beach where you'll find plenty of shops and bars; Panama City is about 60 miles away to the south; Ponce De Leon Springs State Recreation Area is also a few miles to the south; Eden State Gardens are in Panama City Beach. If you like seafood you can try the Sand Flea on Santa Rosa Island. Sam's just across the bridge in Fort Walton Beach has long been famous for its fresh oysters on the half-shell.

RATES: Start at around $25 per night for two persons. Call for confirmation.

OPEN: Year round.

HOW TO GET THERE: From Fort Walton Beach, drive south on Highway 98 to Destin Bridge. From there, drive along 98 for about 10.5 miles to the campground.

Lake Seminole

Three Rivers State Recreation Area

Route 1, Box 15-A, Sneads, FL 32460
(904) 482-9006

The tri-state location, the hardwood and pine forests, the hilly terrain, Lake Seminole, the Flint, the Apalachicola, and the Chatta-hoochee Rivers, all contribute to a setting of unparalleled natural beauty in Florida's Three Rivers Recreation Area. The park is home to a variety of wildlife, making it something of a mecca for nature lovers. White-tailed deer and gray fox roam the woodlands, while squirrels and birds inhabit the treetops. It's a place to retreat from the rigors of daily life, to dream and become one with the wonders of nature. If ever there was a place to get away from it all, this is it.

FACILITIES: There are 65 sites with water and electric hookups and 21 more without hookups at two separate locations; each has a table and grill. The bathhouses are clean and properly maintained. They are handicapped accessible and have flush toilets and hot showers. Youth camping is available, too.

RULES & REGULATIONS: No pets, but guide dogs are welcome. Alcohol and firearms prohibited. Do not feed wild animals.

SECURITY: Very good. Round-the-clock security by a resident park manager. The gates are locked from sunset to 8 AM. Campers are provided with the combination to the gate lock, allowing free exit and access after the park has closed.

NEAREST SERVICES: There's a full-service store in Sneads, less than two miles from the park.

RECREATION: The fishing, both on the lake and on the rivers, is excellent. Lake Seminole is one of the bass capitals of the nation: largemouth and smallmouth bass, catfish, bluegill, speckled perch, shellcracker and bream are only a few of the species that anglers can expect to find in the lake. From water-skiing to canoeing, and from hiking to picnicking, there's something to do for just about everyone. There's a swimming area, a playground, several hiking and nature trails on the property, a boat ramp, and a picnic area. If you don't have a boat, two areas offer lake-side fishing: one from the shore, the other from a dock.

NEARBY ATTRACTIONS: Isolated and remote, set on the shores at the confluence of the three rivers that make up Lake Seminole, there's not much to see or visit in the close vicinity of the park. Florida Caverns State Park is west near Marianna, Falling Waters State Recreation Area is about 40 miles west along Interstate 10, Ponce de Leon Springs State Recreation Area is farther west along Interstate 10. Dead Lakes State Recreation Area is 45 miles south near Wewahitchka on Highway 71. There's a pari-mutuel dog track at Ebro about 55 miles southwest on Highway 79, and Big Bend Jai-Alai pari-mutuel is about 12 miles southeast off Interstate 10 on Highway 270A south.

RATES: $8 per night.

OPEN: Year round.

HOW TO GET THERE: The park is located on Highway 271, two miles north Sneads. From Interstate 10 in Sneads, take Highway 271 North.

Marianna

Florida Caverns State Park

3345 Caverns Road, Marianna, FL 32446
(904) 482-9598

Florida Caverns State Park offers more than the usual recreational facilities. It includes a natural series of connecting caves containing limestone stalactites, stalagmites, columns, rimstone, flowstones, and draperies. Guided tours of the caves conducted by knowledgeable park service guides are quite fascinating.

FACILITIES: There are 32 full-service campsites with water and electric hookups. Each site has a table and grill. The bathhouse is modern, well-maintained, and has flush toilets and hot showers. The restrooms are handicapped accessible. Youth camping facilities are available.

RULES & REGULATIONS: No pets, but guide dogs are welcome. Alcohol and firearms prohibited. Do not feed wild animals.

SECURITY: Very good. Round the clock security by a resident park manager. The gates are locked from sunset to 8 AM. Campers are provided with the combination to the gate lock, allowing free exit and access after the park has closed.

NEAREST SERVICES: Less than two miles away along Highway 166 in Marianna.

RECREATION: There's an equestrian facility north of the park with overnight facilities for horses and several excellent trails. Other popular activities include fishing, canoeing, and boating on the Chipola River, hiking over many miles of excellent trails, bird watching, swimming, and nature study. There's also a visitor center, public swimming areas, a boat ramp, horse trails, and a picnic area.

NEARBY ATTRACTIONS: Falling Waters State Recreation Area is about 20 miles away, west along Interstate 10, Ponce de Leon Springs State Recreation Area is even farther west along Interstate

10, Dead Lakes State Recreation Area is 45 miles south near Wewa-hitchka on Highway 71, and there's a pari-mutuel dog track at Ebro about 35 miles southwest on Highway 79.

RATES: October through February, $8 per night. March through September, $12 per night.

OPEN: Year round.

HOW TO GET THERE: The park is three miles north of Marianna on Highway 167.

Old Town

Suwannee River KOA

PO Box 460, Old Town, FL 32680
(904) 542-7636

The picturesque Suwannee River is the focus of camping here. The river is wide, the vegetation and climate sub-tropical, and the atmosphere one of isolation, peace, and tranquillity. The 50-acre campground is quite small, but your needs are well provided for, both in facilities and on-site recreation. This a place to relax.

FACILITIES: There are 108 large, secluded, shady sites, of which 58 have full-service hookups and 60 have water and electric hook-ups, all to 30 amps; 75 are pull-throughs. There are also a number of one-room Kamping Kabins. The bathhouse is kept in pristine condition and there's always plenty of hot water. The restrooms have flush toilets, the laundry room is modern and well-maintained, and cable TV is available.

RULES & REGULATIONS: Pets are welcome, but must be kept under control at all times. Tenters are welcome, too. The quiet time is 10 PM to 7 AM.

SECURITY: Very good. Handled by on-site staff.

NEAREST SERVICES: There's a full-service grocery store on the property where you can buy most of what you need, but it's always a good idea to stock up on the essentials. There are grocery stores in Cross City and Old Town.

RECREATION: There's a nice recreation room, a large, well-equipped pavilion, and a large swimming pool with lots of pool furniture and plenty of room for sunning. There's also a boat ramp, a fishing dock, and canoes and pontoon boats for rent. Most of the usual court games are available. There are hiking trails for those who enjoy walking. The river is ideal for water-skiing, fishing, boating, and canoeing. In fact, the fishing here is excellent, with plenty of largemouth bass, bream, redbreast sunfish, shellcracker, and catfish. There's also a playground for the kids and a nice picnic area.

RATES: The daily rate for a basic tent site is $16 for two persons. $10-$19 for all other sites ($2.50 per extra camper). One-room Kabins are $25. Children under 17 stay free. Cable TV is supplied free of charge.

OPEN: Year round.

HOW TO GET THERE: From the junction of Highway 19/98/Alt 27, take Highway 349 and drive north for 1½ miles, then turn right.

Panacea & Sopchoppy

Alligator Point Campground

Route 1, Box 3392, Panacea, FL 32346-9714
(904) 349-2525

Alligator Point is a tiny peninsula on the Gulf Coast near Panacea, south of Tallahassee and east of Apalachicola. It's a spot virtually undiscovered by the vacationing public, and never crowded. The campground has been thoughtfully laid out and is beautifully landscaped. It lies right on the ocean, and has plenty to offer.

FACILITIES: Of the 130 available sites, all have full-service hook-ups and picnic tables. Some sites are oceanside, some lakeside. Camping cabins are available for those who prefer a roof overhead but like to do for themselves. Cable TV is available at selected sites. There's a laundry room and a nice bathhouse with lots of hot water.

RULES & REGULATIONS: Pets are welcome, but must be kept on a leash.

SECURITY: The campground is open to the road, but all guests must register RVs, cars and boats, and a careful watch is kept.

NEAREST SERVICES: On site. The campground has the only store on Alligator Point: groceries, RV supplies, and souvenirs. LP gas is available by weight or meter.

RECREATION: There's a large pool, a playground, and a large pavilion. There's a superb clubhouse where there are dances held on weekends and line dancing lessons twice a week. You can play all the usual court games, and the beach is just across the road. You can walk, hike, fish, shell, swim, sunbathe, and beachcomb the hours away without ever leaving the vicinity of the campground, or you can charter a boat and head out to do some serious deep-sea fishing for marlin, sailfish, barracuda, and tuna.

NEARBY ATTRACTIONS: Once again, you'll have to drive if you want to go sightseeing. Tallahassee is north on Highway 319 where you can visit MaClay State Gardens on Thomasville Road, the Knott House Museum on East Park Avenue, the Museum of Florida History at 500 South Bronough Street, the San Luis Archeological and Historic Site (which once was the site of a 17th century Spanish mission), the Tallahassee Museum of History and Natural Science at 3945 Museum Drive, and Wakula Springs State Park at Wakula Springs. The Monticello Historic District is a neat area that spans some 27 blocks at the center of town (located just east of Talla-hassee). Walking tours are available at the Chamber of Commerce at 420 West Washington in Montecello. The coastal town of St. Marks is just a few miles northeast of Alligator Point where you'll find San Marcos De Apalachicola, once a home to pirates, English and Spanish explorers, and Indians. Natural Bridge Battlefield State Historic Site, a Civil War battlefield, is just to the north of Woodville, and you can walk or bicycle the Tallahassee/St. Marks Historic Railroad Trail that runs between the two cities. You'll find many more attractions listed along with the other campgrounds in the region.

RATES: Available on request.

OPEN: Year round.

HOW TO GET THERE: From Tallahassee drive south on Highway 319 to Highway 370 then five miles south on 370 to the campground.

Ochlockonee River State Park

PO Box 5, Sopchoppy, FL 32358
(904) 962-2771

This 392-acre park is an area of outstanding natural beauty on the banks of the Ochlockonee River, at the edge of the Apalachicola National Forest and less than 10 miles from the shores of the Gulf of Mexico. As close as it is to some of Florida's most sophisticated and densely populated areas, the park offers a feeling of remoteness, of a forgotten land though still within easy reach of many attractions.. The shallow grassy wetlands, small ponds, and an amalgam of hard and softwood thickets provide habitats for a diverse mixture of wildlife, including deer, bobcats, foxes, and a wide variety of marine and land-based birds.

FACILITIES: There are 30 full-service campsites with water and electric hookups, picnic tables, and grills. The bathhouse has flush toilets and hot showers, is kept clean and tidy, and handicapped accessible. There is also a laundry room and youth camping facilities.

RULES & REGULATIONS: No pets, but guide dogs are welcome. Alcohol and firearms prohibited in the campground. Do not feed wild animals.

SECURITY: Very good. Round-the-clock security is provided by a resident park manager. The gates are kept locked from sunset to 8 AM. Campers are given the combination to the gate lock, allowing them free exit and access after the park has closed.

NEAREST SERVICES: Less than five miles away, along Highway 377 in Sopchoppy.

RECREATION: There's a swimming area, several nature trails, a boat ramp, showers for public use, and a picnic area. Activities include boating, canoeing, hiking, bird watching, and saltwater and freshwater fishing (largemouth bass, bream, catfish, speckled perch, redfish, and speckled trout).

NEARBY ATTRACTIONS: Tallahassee, is just 45 minutes, or so, north along Highway 369. To the west along Highway 98 lies St. Joseph Peninsula State Recreation Area and the Constitutional Convention State Museum in Port St. Joe.The Constitution Convention State Museum is in Port St. Joe, also along Highway 98; the Lake Jackson Mounds State Archaeological Site is two miles off Interstate 10 in Tallahassee, MaClay State Gardens are a half-mile north of Interstate 10 on Highway 319, and Natural Bridge Battlefield State Historic Site is six miles east of Woodville and 12 miles southeast of Tallahassee off Highway 363. Wakulla Springs State Recreation Area and Lodge is just 14 miles to the south on Highway 267. There's also a pari-mutuel dog track near Monticello on Highway 57/19. The Lake Talquin State Recreation Area is a few miles west of Tallahassee off Interstate 10, the Apalachicola National Forest stretches north and west of the park and Highway 319. St. George Island State Park is on the great barrier island to the east of Apalachicola on Highway 300, and the city and beaches of Apalachicola are just seven miles west on Highway 319/98. The John Gorrie State Museum is on Sixth Street in Apalachicola. The historic little town of St. Marks is about 15 miles east, Alligator Point is just south, and Panacea, "Blue Crab Capital of the World," is next to the park on Highway 98.

RATES: October through February, $8 per night. March through September, $10 per night.

OPEN: Year round.

HOW TO GET THERE: From Tallahassee, take Highway 369 and drive south to its junction with Highway 375. Turn west onto 375. About four miles to Sopchoppy. From Sopchoppy, drive four miles south on US Highway 319.

Panama City Beach

Panama City Beach KOA

8800 Thomas Drive, Panama City Beach, FL 32408
(904) 234-5731

Not a huge campground by Florida's standards, but well-blessed with facilities and opportunities for recreation. Panama City Beach is a mecca for those who love sun, sea and sand. According to experts at the University of Maryland, the nearby St. Andrews State Recreation Area was designated the nation's #1 beach for 1995. The campground is well planned, well run, and scrupulously maintained. The staff is friendly, extremely helpful, and willing to help you plan your stay.

FACILITIES: Of the 116 available sites, 104 have full-service hookups to 50 amps; all sites are paved, 12 are pull-throughs and most have tables. There are several one-room Kamping Kabins, and cable TV is available for a charge; the bathhouse is very clean and there's always plenty of hot water. Sewage disposal is available on site, and there's a modern, well-equipped laundry room.

RULES & REGULATIONS: Pets are welcome but must be kept on a leash at all times. Tenters are welcome.

SECURITY: Excellent: the property is gated and there's a guard on duty as well as staff on site 24 hours.

NEAREST SERVICES: There's a full-service store on the property where you can buy groceries, paper goods, camping supplies, and gasoline. LP gas is also available by weight or meter. Some of Panama City Beach's finest restaurants are only minutes away.

RECREATION: If you're looking for the sun, sea, and sand, this is the place to find it. The city beaches are just 300 yards away, and the nation's finest beach at St. Andrews State Recreation Area is three miles east along Highway 392. If you're a golfer, the lovely Signal Hill Country Club's 18-hole course is right next door. If it's fishing you crave, there's no better spot than Panama City Beach. Charter captains are lined up to take you off-shore, and the County

Pier is north; Dan Russell Pier is a little farther on. For the shopper, there are excellent malls, strip malls, and tiny gift and curiosity shops only minutes away. More opportunities in Panama City itself east on Highway 30 are available. All sorts of watersports are available on the beaches: parasailing, jet-skiing, pedal boats, windsurfing, etc. For the nightlife, you have only to walk across the road to two of the City's finest night clubs. For those who like a little action with their sunshine, there's a pari-mutuel dog track nearby. Boaters will find public access ramps at St. Andrews State Recreation Area.

NEARBY ATTRACTIONS: In Panama City Beach you'll find the Snake-A-Torium Zoo on the Miracle Strip Parkway, the Miracle Strip Amusement Park (also on the Parkway, offers 27 rides, an arcade, and 15 food concession 904-234-5810, under $20), the Gulf World Aquarium where you can see live dolphins, sea lions and tropical birds (at 15412 Front Beach Road, 904-234-5271, under $20), and the Panama Speedway (at 9941 Thomas Drive, 904-234-7007, $5). At the Museum of Man in the Sea you can observe man's endeavors to work, live, and play underwater (has a large number of exhibits, including Sealab, artifacts recovered from wrecks, gold and silver, and some that depict how divers adapt to conditions underwater; 17314 Back Beach Road, 904-235-4101, under $10). Shipwreck Island Water Park is the place to take the kids to enjoy the waterslides and other wet games (12000 Front Beach Road, 800-538-7395, $10 to $20 depending upon the season). In Panama City itself, you might like to visit the Visual Art Center of Northwest Florida where you can view exhibits relating to all areas in the visual arts (19 East Fourth Street, 904 769-4451). You'll find many more attractions listed along with the other campgrounds in the region.

RATES: A basic tent site is $18.95 for two persons per night; a site with full hookups is $22.95 per night for two persons; and a one-room Kamping Kabin is $31.95. Extra person are charged a rate of $2 per person per night. Very busy. Reservations recommended for all seasons.

OPEN: Year round.

HOW TO GET THERE: Westbound – From the junction of Highways 98 and 98ALT (Scenic 98), drive southwest on 98ALT for 1½ miles, then one mile south on Joan Avenue. Turn west onto Thomas Drive (Highway 392) for about ¼ mile to the campground.

Eastbound – From the junction of Highways 98 and 3033, drive ¾ mile south on 3033, then two miles southeast on Highway 392.

St. Andrews State Recreation Area

4415 Thomas Drive, Panama City, FL 32408
(904) 233-5140

St. Andrews, just three miles east of Panama City flanked by St. Andrews Bay and the Gulf of Mexico on the other, is yet another of those state recreation areas with beaches that almost defy description. Rated the number one beach in America for 1995 by Dr. Stephen Leatherman, coastal geologist at the University of Maryland, St. Andrews still remains virtually undiscovered by the vacationing public.

To the west, the shoreline stretches for many miles into the distance, beyond Panama City Beach all the way to Destin and Fort Walton Beach. To the east, just across the inlet, lies Shell Island and more sugar-white sand. It's the sand and the deep, emerald green waters of the Gulf of Mexico, dazzling under the hot Florida sun, that make St. Andrews a unique vacation spot . It's a place for families, children, lovers of the great outdoors, and couples to walk barefoot in the moonlight.

The campground is quite large and can become extremely busy at times. But it's well-managed, and has a range of facilities to be envied by even the most sophisticated of its commercial counterparts.

FACILITIES: Of the 176 sites, all have water and electric hookups to 20 amps, tables and grills. The restrooms are handicapped accessible and the bathhouses have flush toilets and hot showers. Sewage disposal is available for overnight campers only, and there are a number of public telephones on the property.

RULES & REGULATIONS: No pets, but guide dogs are welcome. Alcohol and firearms prohibited. Do not feed wild animals.

SECURITY: Very good. Round-the-clock security by a resident park manager. The gates are locked from sunset to 8 AM. Campers are provided with the combination to the gate lock, allowing free exit and access after the park has closed.

NEAREST SERVICES: There's a grocery store on the property, open April though September, where you can purchase most of the essentials. The shops, restaurants, and supermarkets are only minutes away, either in Panama City Beach or Panama City itself.

RECREATION: Lots to see and do here. There's a large pavilion, a concession shop where you can buy snacks, drinks and candy, a playground, and a public access boat ramp. The nation's number one beach is more than two miles long. From its wide expanse you can swim, surf, fish, and sunbathe. There's also a nature trail where you may encounter all sorts of wild marine birds and animals, including alligators.

Panama City Beach, three miles to the west, is the Panhandle's resort area. For more than 27 miles the beach unrolls in a breathtaking display of natural beauty. And, like many another of Florida's coastal resorts, it claims to be the "Seafood Capital of the World." A diversity of fine and colorful restaurants serves every type of fish and crustacean from fresh amberjack to oysters, and lobster to shark. Aside from the restaurants and cafés, beaches and shops, you'll find plenty more to see and do: golf (Bay Point Resort is next door across the Grand Lagoon), a zoo, amusement parks, museums, and many night clubs and bars.

NEARBY ATTRACTIONS: In Panama City Beach, Gulf World Aquarium is where you can see live dolphins, sea lions, and tropical birds (15412 Front Beach Road, 904-234-5271, under $20). The Panama Speedway (at 9941 Thomas Drive, 904-234-7007, $5), the Museum of Man in the Sea (17314 Back Beach Road, 904-235-4101, under $10), the Snake-A-Torium Zoo on the Miracle Strip Parkway, and the Miracle Strip Amusement Park, also on the Parkway, offers 27 rides, an arcade, and 15 food concessions, (904-234-5810, under $20)are all located here. Shipwreck Island Water Park (12000 Front Beach Road) is the place to take the kids to enjoy the waterslides and other wet games (800-538-7395, $10-$20 depending upon the season). In Panama City itself, you might like to visit the Visual Art Center of Northwest Florida where you can view exhibits relating to all areas in the visual arts (19 East Fourth Street, 904-769-4451).

RATES: October through February, $8 per night. March through September, $15 per night.

OPEN: Year round.

HOW TO GET THERE: From the junction of Highway 98 and Thomas Drive, go 3½ miles south on Thomas Drive, then ¼ mile southeast.

Pensacola

Adventures Unlimited

Route 6, Box 283, Milton, FL 32570
(904) 623-6197

Tomahawk Landing, an 88-acre park at the confluence of the Coldwater River and Wolfe Creek, is the headquarters for Adventures Unlimited Canoeing. Cutting across the Panhandle at regular intervals, a series of clear forested rivers, their banks dotted with broad expanses of white sand, provide some of the best canoeing and camping in the United States. For something different, you'll find this outdoor adventure company and campground just what you're looking for. The camping facilities are limited, so you'll have to book early, but what is available is well-managed and kept very clean and tidy, the emphasis being on recreation.

Historic Pensacola village.

FACILITIES: Of the 25 available sites, 17 have water and electric hookups to 50 amps; eight are pull-throughs. There are also several rental cabins on the property. The bathhouse has flush toilets, showers, and plenty of hot water. Sewage disposal is available for guests only. There are public telephones available on-site.

RULES & REGULATIONS: No pets. Tenters are welcome.

SECURITY: The remote location and the presence of on-site staff effectively eliminate any potential security problems.

NEAREST SERVICES: There's a limited grocery store on the property, but you'd be well advised to stock up on the essentials before you arrive. Milton is about 16 miles away to the south.

RECREATION: This is a family resort where the focus is on canoeing and the great outdoors. Facilities on the property include a recreation hall, a playground for the kids, nature trails, hiking trails, bicycling trails, picnic shelters, campfire circles. On the water lots of opportunities for fishing, boating, rafting, and, of course, canoeing. There are 400 canoes for rental, and the staff routinely conducts canoeing lessons and overnight camping trips up-river. Pedal boats are also available for rent, and there are the usual court games: volleyball, horseshoes, etc.

The National Museum of Naval Aviation in Pensacola.

NEARBY ATTRACTIONS: Milton is just down the road, but it's a typical rural small town. Pensacola, some 30 miles to the south on Highway 90, is the nearest big city to the campground. There you'll find the attractions, restaurants, night clubs, shops, and beaches of the Gulf Islands National Seashore. The National Museum of Naval Aviation, one of the three largest air and space museums in the world is here. It traces the history and development of Navy, Marine Corps, and Coast Guard aviation through exhibits that include almost 100 authentic and historic aircraft from blimps to biplanes to space-age aircraft and the Skylab Command Module (Building 3465, Naval Air Station, Pensacola, 904-453-NAVY; admission is free). The T.T. Wentworth, Jr., Florida State Museum (330 South Jefferson in Pensacola) is a restored Mediterranean Revival city hall that now houses a collection of fascinating objects and memorabilia on the history and development of West Florida, including the Hygeia Bottling Company Coca Cola Collection (904-444-8586; admission is $5). The North Hill Preservation District, also in Pensacola, is on the National Register of Historic Places and is well worth a visit. Developed as an upper-class neighborhood between 1870 and 1930, it reflects the architectural fashions of pre-World War II Pensacola. No visit to the Pensacola area would be complete without a day trip to either Perdido Key or Santa Rosa Island, where you can enjoy the sea and sand on Pensacola Beach. Along the coast to the east lie Fort Walton Beach, Destin, and a dozen or so more small seaside towns that dot the Gulf shores all the way to Panama City Beach – all quaint little places where you can go for sea and sand, golf, and deep sea fishing.

RATES: Rates for camping start at around $12 per night for two persons. Call for canoe/camping package rates.

OPEN: Year round.

HOW TO GET THERE: From the junction of US 90 and Highway 87 in Milton, drive north on Highway 87 for about 12 miles, then follow the signs east for about four miles to the campground.

Big Lagoon State Recreation Area

12301 Gulf Beach Highway, Pensacola, FL 32507
(904) 492-1592

Big Lagoon, complete with observation tower, is a bird watcher's paradise. The park provides habitats for many species of land and water birds: nuthatches, cardinals, the great blue heron, and many more. It's an area where wide sandy beaches and great salt marshes meld with the Gulf Islands National Seashore and the Intracoastal Waterway. The campground is, as all of Florida's state parks are, well planned and maintained with helpful staff to answer questions about wildlife and habitat.

FACILITIES: There are 75 full-service campsites with water and electric hookups, tables and grills. The bathhouse has flush toilets, hot showers and most facilities are handicapped accessible. Sewage disposal is available for campers only.

RULES & REGULATIONS: No pets, but guide dogs are welcome. Alcohol and firearms prohibited. Do not feed wild animals.

SECURITY: Very good. Round-the-clock security by a resident park manager. The gates are locked from sunset to 8 AM. Campers are provided with the combination to the gate lock, allowing free exit and access after the park has closed.

NEAREST SERVICES: There are a number of convenience stores in Chanticleer within walking distance of the park. The big stores, supermarkets and restaurants are less than 10 miles away in Pensacola.

RECREATION: Located on the Gulf Islands National Seashore, it's no wonder that recreation revolves around the sea, sand, and wildlife. There's a large pavilion with meeting rooms on the property, boat ramps and swimming, a picnic area, and, of course, the observation tower for bird watching. Activities include pond and saltwater fishing, boating, canoeing, hiking along the beach and nature trails, picnicking, swimming, and bird and nature study.

NEARBY ATTRACTIONS: Gulf Islands National Seashore, the Zoo and Botanical Gardens (5701 Gulf Breeze Parkway in Gulf Breeze, 904-932-2229, $5); Gulf Breeze Fishing Pier (3 Mile Bridge, 904-934-5147, under $5); Bay Bluffs Park (Highway 90 at Summit Boulevard in Pensacola, 1-800-874-1234, admission is free); the Pensacola Beach Fishing Pier just down the road to the east (Fort Pickens Road at Casino Beach, 904-932-0444, $5); and the Art Center and Wentworth Museum (330 South Jefferson Street in Pensacola, 904-444-8586, $5). You'll find many more attractions listed along with the other campgrounds in the region.

RATES: $8 per night.

OPEN: Year round.

HOW TO GET THERE: The park is on CR 292A, about 10 miles to the southwest of Pensacola. From Pensacola, drive southwest on Highway 292 to its junction with 292A, turn east onto 292A and drive about two miles to the park.

Port St. Joe

Cape San Blas Camping Resort

PO Box 645, Port St. Joe, FL 32456
(904) 229-6800

Cape San Blas on the southern shores of St. Joseph Bay seems to be just about as far away from everywhere as you can get. It's a desolate land where only the sounds of the sea rolling in over the sugar white sand and the raucous call of the seabirds swooping and diving in search of the next meal disturb the quiet of the great outdoors. Dolphins play in the waters off-shore, and pompano and snapper wait for fishermen to cast their lines. Cape San Blas was recently acclaimed one of the top five beaches in the United States, according to a study by the University of Maryland. More than 20 miles of white, sandy beaches form a natural habitat of magnificent dunes and waving seagrass, hugging the emerald green waters of the Gulf of Mexico. St. Joe is a relatively undiscovered region of Northwest Florida where the favorite pastimes are fishing, swimming, snorkeling and water-skiing. The camp is located 20 minutes from Port St. Joe and Mexico Beach. The fishing is claimed to be the best on the Gulf Coast: cobia, bluefish, and snapper in vast quantities inhabit the waters just off the beaches. Farther out, live the great game fish: marlin, sailfish and tuna. For the golfer, or those who might prefer a set or two of tennis, St. Joseph's Bay Country Club is just five minutes away, and all the nightlife you can handle is less than an hour to the north in Panama City.

The camping resort, though small by most standards, is all you might expect of one in such a location. The facilities are also a little limited, but what it lacks in the basics it more than makes up for in aesthetics, recreation, and service.

FACILITIES: There are just 46 sites with room for RVs of 36 feet or less. Only four sites have full-service hookups, 29 have water and electric hookups, while the remaining 13 have no hookups at all. Having said that, you do have a choice of sites either with rustic shelters or among the shady palms and pines. All sites have picnic tables, and fire rings are located on the beach in selected areas. Water is supplied by the municipal system. Hot showers in the restrooms near the beach and pool areas are provided at no extra charge. All members of the staff can communicate in sign language. There are a number of rental cabins available.

RULES & REGULATIONS: Pets are welcome.

SECURITY: Very good, provided by on-site staff.

NEAREST SERVICES: There is a camp store where you can buy groceries, ice, cold beverages, camping supplies, paper goods, and fishing tackle. The shops and supermarkets of Port St. Joe are just 10 miles away.

RECREATION: If you love the beach and the ocean, this is the place for you. Recently designated one of the top five beaches in the nations, you'll find more than two miles of undeveloped sugar white sand set aside just for you to enjoy. You can go surf fishing, crabbing, scallop and oyster gathering, shelling, swimming and sunbathing. Deep sea fishing charters out of Apalachicola and Mexico Beach can be arranged by the staff. St. Joseph's Bay Country Club will welcome you to play it's challenging 18-hole, championship golf course or make use of the tennis courts. Back on the property, there's a large swimming pool, rowing and sailing boats and canoes for rent, and the usual assortment of court games. For nightlife you can head out to Panama City.

St. Vincent Island Wildlife Refuge is a short distance away. You can easily make the trip by canoe rented on property. Once there, you'll see all sorts of wildlife, including rare ocean birds, wild hogs, deer, and alligators.

NEARBY ATTRACTIONS: The emphasis here is placed very much on the beaches and the peninsula, but if you're prepared to travel a little, you can visit the Museum of Man in the Sea or Shipwreck Island Water Park in Panama City. Apalachicola is east, Fort Gadsden State Historic Site is at Marianna,Dead Lakes State Recreation Area at Wewahitchka, and the St. Joseph's Peninsula State Park is just down the road to the west.

RATES: Very reasonable. They range from $10-$14, depending upon whether you're located on the beach or at poolside, and the facilities available at the site.

OPEN: Year round.

HOW TO GET THERE: From the junction of Highways 71 and 98, drive two miles east on 98 to Highway 30. Take Highway 30 and drive south for seven miles to Cape San Blas Road. From there you'll drive west for about 1½ miles to the campground.

St. Joseph Peninsula

Rustic Sands Resort Campground

HC03 800 North 15th Street, Mexico Beach, FL 32456
(904) 648-5229

Location, according to those who make a living in real estate, is the all important consideration when buying a home. Many people would say it's also the most important consideration when choosing a vacation spot, and, if that's true, Rustic Sands must be the perfect holiday destination; it's certainly the reason this very small campground is included here. It's neat, secluded, shaded, extremely well-kept and maintained, and the service provided by the staff is excellent. If you want to get away to an idyllic, romantic setting, Rustic Sands is probably what you're looking for.

FACILITIES: The management has given up quantity for quality. The 48 sites are all large, but only 22 have full-service hookups to 30 amps; the other 26 sites have water and electric hookups, and 12 are pull-throughs. The campground has city water services. The bathhouse has flush toilets and hot showers. Sewage disposal is available. There's a modern, well-equipped laundry room, and public phones are available on the property.

RULES & REGULATIONS: Tenters are welcome. Pets are welcome so long as they are not too big and are kept under control at all times. The quiet time is 10 PM until 7 AM.

SECURITY: Good. Handled by on-site staff.

NEAREST SERVICES: There's a store on the property, but it's a small one, so you would be well-advised to stock up on hard-to-get items before you arrive. There are convenience stores and supermarkets close at hand in Mexico Beach, and more just south in Port St. Joe.

RECREATION: The emphasis here is on the location, the beaches, and peace and quiet. Rustic Sands is only a couple of minutes away from some of the finest beaches on the Gulf Coast. On the property there's a unique recreation hall, a pond for fishing, and all the usual court and ball games. There's a marina and boat ramps less than a mile away and, if you like pier fishing, Mexico Beach Fishing Pier is also less than a mile away.

NEARBY ATTRACTIONS: St. Joseph Peninsula State Recreation Area is just a few miles south on Highway 98, and the Constitution Convention State Museum is in Port St. Joe, also along Highway 98. Besides local attractions in Mexico Beach and Port St. Joe, you'll have to travel to do your sightseeing. Florida's state capital, Tallahassee, is about 80 miles north along Highway 98, but it's a very nice drive. Natural Bridge Battlefield State Historic Site is six miles east of Woodville and 12 miles southeast of Tallahassee off Highway 363. Wakulla Springs State Recreation Area and Lodge is just 14 miles south on Highway 267. There's a pari-mutuel dog track near Monticello on Highway 57/19. The city and beaches of Apalachicola are 30 miles southeast on Highway 98. The John Gorrie State Museum is on Sixth Street in Apalachicola. The Apalachicola National Forest stretches to the north of Apalachicola; St. George Island is just east of Apalachicola; Ochlockonee River State Park is northeast of St. George on Highway 98; Alligator Point is close by; and the historic little town of St. Marks is also on the coast to the east. Panacea, "Blue Crab Capital of the World," is to the northeast of Apalachicola on Highway 98.

RATES: Extremely reasonable. Sites around $15 per night for two persons.

OPEN: Year round.

HOW TO GET THERE: From Mexico Beach's center, drive one mile east on Highway 98, then ¾ mile north on North 15th Street.

St. Joseph Peninsula State Park

S.R. 1, Box 200, Port St. Joe, FL 32456
(904) 227-1327

St. Joseph Peninsula State Park offers 2,500 acres of fun. Located on a long, thin strip of beach and surrounded on three sides by the Gulf of Mexico and St. Joseph's Bay, it's a park with a difference. St. Joseph is also rated as one of the nation's top 10 beaches by Dr. Stephen Leatherman, coastal geologist at the University of Maryland. The pale green ocean has some of the best swimming and snorkeling anywhere in Florida. And, with sightings of 209 species of wild birds, it's one of the best bird watching spots in the United States, especially for watching the annual fall migration of hawks.

FACILITIES: Of the 119 sites on two campgrounds, 79 have water and electric hookups, 40 have no hookups, and all have picnic tables. There are seven fully-furnished vacation cabins, all on the shores of St. Joseph Bay, complete with private kitchens and bathrooms. The restrooms are handicapped accessible and the bathhouses have flush toilets and hot showers. Sewage disposal is available only to overnight campers. There are cold water showers on the beach, and a number of public telephones – some at the campsites, some near the store. A youth camping facility for use by non-profit groups is available.

RULES & REGULATIONS: No pets, but guide dogs are welcome. Alcohol and firearms prohibited. Do not feed wild animals.

SECURITY: Very good. Round-the-clock security by a resident park manager. The gates are locked from sunset to 8 AM. Campers are provided with the combination to the gate lock,allowing free exit and access after the park has closed.

NEAREST SERVICES: There's a grocery store on the property where you can buy most of what you need, as well as fishing supplies and other sundry items. The shops and supermarkets of Port St. Joe are just 16 miles across the bay via Highways 30E & A.

RECREATION: There's a boat ramp and marina on the property where you can rent canoes. There are also several hiking trails, as well as the many miles of beach, and a 1,600-acre wilderness area where you can go for long walks. Fishing, a major pastime at St. Joseph's, and you can be done from the shore either in the Gulf or

St. Joseph's Bay. You can do some bird watching, go swimming (there are freshwater showers on the beach), snorkeling, or sunbathing. Of special interest are the nature programs, guided walks through the wilderness area, and campfire programs conducted by park service personnel.

NEARBY ATTRACTIONS: The focus of this park is on the beaches, the peninsula, and Port St. Joe, where you'll find the Constitution Convention State Museum (15412 Front Beach Road). Beyond that, Panama City is 35 miles northwest from Port St. Joe via Highway 98. Gulf World Aquarium is where you can see live dolphins, sea lions, and tropical birds (904-234-5271, under $20). The Panama Speedway (9941 Thomas Drive, 904-234-7007, $5), the Museum of Man in the Sea (17314 Back Beach Road, 904-235-4101, under $10), the Snake-A-Torium Zoo, and the Miracle Strip Amusement Park, both on the Parkway, offers 27 rides, an arcade, and 15 food concessions, (904-234-5810, under $20). The Shipwreck Island Water Park (at 12000 Front Beach Road) is also here.

Apalachicola and its beaches lie to the east . The John Gorrie State Museum is on Sixth Street in Apalachicola. Beyond Apalachicola you'll find the Ochlockonee River State Park on Highway 98, Alligator Point is even closer to the northeast, and St. Marks is about 20 miles to the east. Panacea is also to the northeast on Highway 98, and the Apalachicola National Forest stretches north.

RATES: The rates for camping November through February are $8 per night; March through October, $15 per night. For vacation cabins March 1st through September 15th the rate is $70 per night; from September 16th through February it's $55.

OPEN: Year round.

HOW TO GET THERE: From the junction of Highways 71 and 98, drive south for nine miles on 98 to Highway 30. Turn west on 30 and drive on for four miles to Highway 30E. Turn north on 30E and drive nine miles to the park.

Suwannee

Miller's Marine

PO Box 280, Suwannee, FL 32692-0280
(800) 458-BOAT

For a change you might want to try this unique campground set on
the banks of one of Florida's most scenic rivers. The Suwannee is
still one of the state's least used waterways, and Miller's can provide a vacation you're not likely to forget. The campground is a
small one, but it's neat, clean, and appealing. It's the river and the
way the Millers have put it to use that qualifies the campground for
inclusion here. You can either go camping the conventional way, or
you can park your RV, trailer, or tent, and step aboard a 44-foot
houseboat and cruise the river for a weekend or more. Long lazy
days and dreamy starlit nights, fishing on the river, sunning, or just
relaxing in the luxury of a small floating house, complete with
shower and flush toilets, all make for a different type of experience.

FACILITIES: There are 41 waterfront sites, all with full-service
hookups, cable TV and picnic tables. There are also several cabins
and 70 houseboats for rent by day or week. The bathhouse is clean
and there's plenty of hot water for showers around the clock. The
laundry room is modern and well maintained.

RULES & REGULATIONS: Pets are welcome. Tenters are welcome, too.

SECURITY: Good. Handled by on-site staff.

NEAREST SERVICES: Just minutes away in Suwannee.

RECREATION: If you're looking for lots of sightseeing, nightlife
and action, this is not the place for you. The campground is in a
remote area of the upper Gulf coast, far from the crowded resorts
and beaches. Here you can spend time in almost splendid isolation.
Fishing, walking, bicycling, canoeing, boating, photography, bird
watching and the like are all popular pastimes, but a two-day trip
up the river on a houseboat is perhaps the most appealing experience. If you have a boat, you'll find the marina can look after most

of your needs, including gasoline. There's a boat ramp to provide access to the river, and you can rent a slip or put your boat into storage. You can also rent a fishing boat, canoe, or bicycle. Fishing on the river and in the Gulf of Mexico is excellent: lots of large-mouth bass, sunfish, shellcracker, redbreast, and catfish.

RATES: Campsites are $12 to $17 per day for two persons; extra persons $2 each. Cabins $55 per day for two persons; extra persons $5 each. House boat rates, depending on the season, are $296 to $446 for two days and the rates rise accordingly for each extra day, with the seventh day free.

OPEN: Year round.

HOW TO GET THERE: Take Highway 19/27 to its junction with Highway 349. Turn south on 349.

Central East Coast

This has long been one of Florida's most popular coastal areas. Almost every vacation experience you can imagine is available, from the excitement of the great rockets blasting off into the unknown from the Space Coast, the thrills of high-speed motor-racing at Daytona, sunken pirate's gold on the beaches of the Treasure Coast, the fabulous beaches themselves, to the abundant wildlife in the great refuges and wetlands.

Daytona is the big town on Florida's East Coast. For many years it's been second only to Indianapolis as far as motor racing fans are concerned, and every year they descend on the city and its International Speedway in hundreds of thousands. Daytona is more than a racetrack. The beaches are world famous. Daytona is also a major cultural center with a number of fine museums, theaters, and historical sites.

A little farther to the south, beyond Port Orange and New Smyrna, Florida's Space Coast tops the list of spectacular attractions. From the Kennedy Space Center to Spaceport USA and the US Astronaut Hall of Fame, visitors to this section of the coast are treated to an array of tradition, patriotism, excitement and the wonders of a dozen or more museums, theaters, galleries, and exhibits. Just to the east, the Canaveral National Seashore and Merritt Island National Wildlife Refuge offer not only a wild and lonely area of great natural beauty to explore, but a vast natural habitat for hundreds of species of wildlife, including seabirds and turtles.

To the south, the counties of Indian River and St. Lucie have become famous as America's Treasure Coast. It was here that the great Spanish treasure fleets, plying the heavy seas eastward to Cadiz laden with gold, silver, and gems, were swept northward by hurricanes and lost on the rocks. And it's here that treasure seekers, beachcombers, anglers, and those who just need a little peace and quiet, come to spend pleasant hours in the sunshine. The opportunities for outdoor recreation are unparalleled on the Treasure Coast. Diving, snorkeling, golfing, tennis, hiking, nature watching, dining, and baseball – this is where the Dodgers, Mets, Marlins and Astros hold their spring training – are just a few of the possibilities that await.

Indian River is where the early settlers built their homes and vast plantations. Today, the river is just as beautiful and enticing as it was all those hundreds of years ago. Visitors come from around the nation to enjoy the area. The fishing is superb, the scenery dazzling, and the magnificent off-shore reefs are a magnet for divers and snorkellers. If you like to windsurf, sail, boat, or fish, this is the place for you.

Vero Beach is another pleasant spot on the east coast, but is still virtually undiscovered by the great vacationing multitudes. For those who know, it's a favorite spot to avoid the crowds, enjoy the peaceful sandy beaches, fine restaurants, and outstanding shopping centers. It remains one of few unspoiled areas on the central east coast.

Stuart is the sport fishing capital of east Florida. It's a little town with a big reputation among the aficionados who know all about such things. It's a quaint little place where there seem to be more fishing boats than homes. The sun goes down nightly over the harbor in a blaze of red and gold and sets the atmosphere for a night of quiet reminiscence after a day on the ocean in search of the "big one."

Hobe Sound and Jensen Beach are Florida's favorite turtle spotting locations. During June and July, thousands flock to the warm sands to join ranger-led nighttime expeditions and watch the loggerhead turtles' annual migration from sea to sand.

Cocoa Beach

Oceanus Mobile Village & RV Resort

152 Crescent Beach Drive (23rd Street), Cocoa Beach, FL 32931
(407) 783-3871

It's the beautiful location that earned this laid-back little camp-ground a place in this book. Situated on a narrow strip of land between the river and the ocean, just 30 minutes from the Kennedy Space Center, visitors can enjoy views from the campground of the space shuttle blasting off.

FACILITIES: All the sites have full-service hookups, trailers are available for rent, the bathhouses have all the usual facilities, and tenters are welcome. There's also a laundry room, a heated swim-ming pool and spa, pets are welcome if kept on a leash, and access to the water is available via on-site boat slips.

SECURITY: Handled by the live-in owner and campground staff.

NEAREST SERVICES: If there is a criticism it would be the lack of an on-site store. You can stock up before you arrive and there's a grocery store three miles away. There's a small mall just five miles away, and Merritt Square Mall, a very large shopping center, is just 10 miles from the campground. A restaurant is located on the grounds.

RECREATION: There's lots to see and do: the fishing is great, the beaches even better, water sports are premium, and the setting is perfect for a relaxing vacation, not too far away from the action, but far enough to provide a sense of isolation in the great outdoors. There's a restaurant on the premises, the beach is only 200 feet away, and a 240-foot-long pier provides fishing in the good old fashioned way – or you can just relax and enjoy the view.

NEARBY ATTRACTIONS: Cape Canaveral is, of course, the main attraction on this part of the east coast. At Titusville, the US Astro-naut Hall Of Fame, just west of the Kennedy Space Center (open from 9 AM-5 PM daily) is the place to go for a trip to the stars aboard a full-scale model of an orbiter. The US Space Camp (6225

The Ron Jon Surf Shop at Cocoa Beach.

Vector Boulevard in Titusville, 9 AM-5 PM daily) is just the setting for youngsters, 4th through 7th grades, to explore the wonders of space travel. The Kennedy Space Center is also in Titusville. Two-hour tours of the Center are conducted throughout the day, and you can view the complimentary IMAX movies "The Dream is Alive" and "The Blue Planet." The Space Center is open daily from 9 AM until dusk and a visit will take at least six hours if you want to "do it properly." Nearby Cocoa Beach Pier has the only restaurants, bars, and shops located 800 feet over the Atlantic Ocean. The pier is a complete entertainment complex and is open daily from 6 AM until 2 AM. The restaurants open for lunch at 11 AM.

RATES: Call for rates.

HOW TO GET THERE: The campground is 5½ miles south of the 520 Causeway on Highway A1A, and one mile north of Patrick Air Force Base.

Daytona Beach

Daytona Beach Campground

4601 Clyde Morris Boulevard, Daytona Beach, FL 32119
(904) 761-2663

Although it's not as large as some on the east coast, Daytona Beach campground is close to most of the action, only 10 minutes away from one of the most famous beaches in the world, and has a friendly staff to make sure you're welcome, settled down, and want for nothing.

FACILITIES: Of the 180 available sites, more than half have full-service hookups, the rest have water and electric, cable TV and telephone hookups are available at extra charge. The bathhouses are well-maintained and provide all the usual amenities, including plenty of hot water. There's also a laundry room, and sewage disposal is available for overnight campers.

RULES & REGULATIONS: No tents, pets allowed only if kept under tight control. The quiet time is 10 PM to 7 AM.

SECURITY: Good. Provided by on-site staff.

NEAREST SERVICES: There's a full-service store where you can purchase most of your basic needs, including LP gas by weight or meter. There are large supermarkets just down the road in Daytona.

RECREATION: Facilities include a fully-equipped recreation hall, a 50-foot heated swimming pool with lots of room for sunbathing, a kiddy pool, playground, and a number of court games. The staff provides a program of planned group activities during the winter months, and there are a number of local tour operators to show you the sights. The campground is 10 minutes away from the beach, International Speedway, Jai Alai, golf course, fishing pier, and the dog track. There's regular bus service into the city.

NEARBY ATTRACTIONS: There's always lots to see and do in and around Daytona Beach. The beach itself is a must, as is the International Speedway. Beyond that there's the Gamble Place Historic House Museum (1040 Museum Boulevard), Halifax Historical Museum (252 South Beach Street), the Museum of Arts and Sciences (Museum Boulevard), and the Planetarium at the Museum of Arts and Sciences. The International Speedway Welcome Center (1801 West International Speedway Boulevard) offers tours. Outside of Daytona you might want to visit the Casemates at Ormond Beach, Tomoka State Park, the Bulow Plantation Ruins, Flagler Beach, Sugar Mill Gardens, De Leon Springs State Park, and the Canaveral National Seashore. All are just a short drive away from the campground.

RATES: From $20 for two persons.

OPEN: Year round. Very busy. Reservations are a must for all seasons.

HOW TO GET THERE: From Exit 86A on Interstate 95, drive 2½ miles east on Highway 400, then 3½ miles south on Clyde Morris Boulevard.

Fort Pierce

Road Runner Travel Resort

5500 St. Lucie Boulevard, Ft. Pierce, FL 34946
(407) 464-0969

Fort Pierce in St. Lucie County is something of a forgotten jewel on Florida's Atlantic coast. It's an area of natural beauty, lakes, sea islands, beaches, golf courses, parks, and a center for deep-sea sportfishing. Often a little quieter than many of its neighboring resort communities, Fort Pierce is an ideal spot to relax for a few days, but not so far away that you'll feel isolated and out of touch. Sited on a 38-acre hammock amid attractive countryside, Road Runner is just four miles from the beaches. It's busy, yet quiet, well-laid out, and well-managed with lots of facilities and opportunities for recreation and relaxation.

FACILITIES: Of the 450 available sites, all have full-service hookups, but only 40 are pull-throughs; if you must have a pull-through you'll need to make your reservations early. Telephone hookups are available. There are two bathhouses – one large and handicapped accessible. Sewage disposal is available to overnight campers, and there's a large, well-equipped laundry room. RVs are available for rent.

RULES & REGULATIONS: Pets are allowed but must be kept on a leash at all times; no barking or vicious dogs. Children should also be kept under control. The quiet time is 10 PM until 7 AM.

SECURITY: Excellent. The park is gated and locked when the store closes; passes are issued to guests. The guard will allow no one through without a pass.

NEAREST SERVICES: There's a full-service store on site where you can get most of what you need. Propane is available by weight or meter. There's also a nice restaurant open during the winter months.

RECREATION: The campground is well-equipped with recreational facilities. There's a large pool with a nice patio for sunning, a pavilion, recreation hall, two tennis courts, a number of other court games, and a small lake where you can fish. The emphasis here, because the beaches and shops at Fort Pierce are some distance away, is on the surrounding countryside and Lake Okeechobee, where you can fish, sail, canoe, swim, hike, and picnic.

NEARBY ATTRACTIONS: The St. Lucie County Historical Museum (414 Seaway Drive in Fort Pierce) is worth a visit, as are the Heathcote Botanical Gardens (210 Savannah Road), the Harbor Branch Oceanographic Institute (5600 North US1), the IRCC Planetarium, the Indian River Memorial Park, and the Savannas Recreation Area on Midway Road where you can enjoy nature at its best: hiking, freshwater fishing, canoe rentals, bird watching, and so on.

RATES: Very reasonable at $21 per night for two persons and $2 per extra person per night.

OPEN: Year round.

HOW TO GET THERE: From Exit 66B on Interstate 95, drive ½ mile west on Highway 68, then 3½ miles north on Highway 713, then .3 miles east on CR 608.

Jupiter

Jupiter, just to the east of Lake Okeechobee, is the oldest settlement in Palm Beach County. Founded as a fort in 1838 during the Seminole Indian Wars, it's famous for its lighthouse, theater, beaches, and Jupiter Island Park.

Juno Beach RV Resort

900 Juno Ocean Walk, Juno Beach, FL 33408-1107
(407) 622-7500

Juno Beach is just a few miles south of Jupiter and is consistently rated among the top commercial campgrounds in the state by

Trailer World. The facilities for camping and recreation are extensive; it's a resort in every sense of the word.

FACILITIES: There are 246 large sites, all with paved pads and full-service hookups (water, electric, sewer and telephone, if required) to 50 amps. The restrooms and bathhouses are handicapped accessible, have hot showers and flush toilets, and are clean and well-maintained. Sewage disposal is available for overnight guests only. There's a modern, well-equipped laundry room, and a number of public telephones at convenient locations.

RULES & REGULATIONS: Pets are welcome, but must be kept on a leash. No tents or pop-up trailers. The quiet time is 10 PM to 7 AM.

SECURITY: Very good. Handled by on-site staff.

NEAREST SERVICES: There's a plaza and grocery store adjacent to the campground.

RECREATION: There's a recreation hall on the property, a heated swimming pool with lots of room for relaxing and sunbathing, all the usual court games, a fishing pond and a playground. A full-time recreation director is on hand to look after all your needs and organize a full program of activities during the winter months. The beaches, restaurants (be sure to give the Jupiter Crab Company a try), and shops are just a short walk away.

NEARBY ATTRACTIONS: The Jupiter Theater (1001 East Indiantown Road in Jupiter) offers a range of seating from showroom to dining status to VIP skyboxes and a full program of entertainment for adults and children (call for schedule and rates, 407-746-5566). The Marinelife Center of Juno Beach is at 1200 Highway 1. Loggerhead Park, in Juno Beach, is where you see the aquariums, view the exhibits, turtles and other wildlife, or attend a lecture (free; open Tuesday–Saturday, 10 AM-4 PM, noon-3 PM Sunday; 407-627-8280). You might also like to visit the Dreher Park Zoo (1301 Summit Boulevard in West Palm Beach), where you can stroll the 22-acre park and see more than 500 exotic and domestic animals in natural settings (open 9 AM-5 PM daily; less than $5; 407-533-0887).

RATES: Start at around $35 per night for two persons. The campground is often very busy, so be sure to book your site as far in advance as you can.

OPEN: Year round.

HOW TO GET THERE: 1
US 1, drive two miles sout.

114 Central East Coast

FACILITIES: There are 51 p
and picnic tables. The b
and is handicapped
picnic area, sever
showers are av

RULES
Alcol

$M\epsilon$

Sabastian Inlet St

9700 South A1A, N.
(407) 9t

If you are a saltwater angler, you'll find no finer location for your sport than the Sabastian Inlet State Recreation Area. This park transports visitors back to the days when the Spanish treasure fleets turned eastward toward Europe and their home port of Cadiz. It was close to the Sabastian Inlet, in 1715, that a hurricane caused the wreck of an entire fleet of galleons returning to Spain from Mexico and Peru. The survivors of the catastrophe swam ashore and made camp some 1½ miles to the south of the inlet. Today, on the site of the survivor's camp, the McLarty Treasure Museum houses a wealth of exhibits that tell the story of the shipwreck, the early attempts to salvage the treasure, and many artifacts and valuable objects recovered during later expeditions. The museum also features a slide show presenting the natural and cultural history of the area.

The park itself is on one of the many barrier islands that protect Florida's southeastern shoreline from the ravages of nature. It's a complex world of sandy beaches, dunes, coastal hammocks, bordered mangroves and forests that provide, not only important habitats for the wildlife community, but one of Florida's finest recreational facilities.

The Sabastian Inlet itself and the surrounding Atlantic waters offer some of the finest saltwater fishing, shrimping, and clamming in the state. There are two Atlantic jetties, catwalks under the Inlet bridge, more than three miles of beaches, and the Indian River, giving access to an abundance of snook, redfish, bluefish, and Spanish mackerel.

..s, all with water and electric hookups
..house has flush toilets and hot showers
..cessible. There's a boat ramp and dock, a
.. sites where public restrooms and fresh water
..lable, plus parking facilities.

.. REGULATIONS: No pets, but guide dogs are welcome.
..ol and firearms prohibited. Do not feed wild animals.

SECURITY: Very good. Round-the-clock security by a resident park manager. The gates are locked from sunset to 8 AM. Campers are provided with the combination to the gate lock, allowing free exit and access after the park has closed.

NEAREST SERVICES: There's a concession facility on the property that serves breakfast and lunch daily, and where you can buy a variety of camping and fishing supplies, rent beach chairs and fishing equipment. There's a Publix supermarket about eight miles north on Highway A1A.

RECREATION: Activities include swimming, snorkeling, scuba diving, hiking the miles of sandy beaches, sunning, windsurfing, fishing, boating, bird watching, and nature study. The park offers a rare opportunity to observe the osprey, many species of shore and wading birds, sea turtles, and, at times, the manatee. The Sabastian Inlet is regarded as one of the finest surfing sites on the entire Atlantic coast, hosting several national surfing tournaments each year. Of special interest, during the months of June and July, are the nighttime, ranger-led expeditions in search of nesting loggerhead turtles. If you want to join such an excursion, you'll need to contact the ranger station and make a reservation.

NEARBY ATTRACTIONS: Lake Griffin State Recreation Area, Lake Griffin, Lake Harris, Merritt Island, Lake Eustis, Lake Apopka, Walt Disney World at Orlando, Wikiwa Springs State Park, Rock Springs Run State Reserve, Dade Battlefield State Historic Site, the Fort Mellon Historic Site, the Ben White Raceway at Orlando, Lake Louisa State Recreation Area, the Mead Botanical Gardens at Orlando, Clearwater Lake, the Ocala National Forest, the Early American Museum at Silver Springs, the Reptile Institute at Silver Springs, Silver Springs Wildwater, Hontoon Island State Park, Port St. Lucie, Stuart, Hobe Sound, the Jupiter Lighthouse, the John D. MacArthur Beach State Park, the St. Lucie Lock and Dam, Vero Beach, Lake Okeechobee, the St. Lucie Inlet State Preserve, the Elliott Museum, Jupiter Sound, Hobe Sound National

Wildlife Refuge, and the Blowing Rocks Reserve. The entire area surrounding Sabastian Inlet offers unlimited adventures. To name them all would be impossible, but the above list should give you lots of ideas.

RATES: May through November, $15 per night. December through April, $17 per night.

OPEN: Year round.

HOW TO GET THERE: From the junction of Highways 510 and A1A, drive north for seven miles on A1A.

Ormond Beach

Ocean Village Camper Resort

2162 Ocean Shore Blvd., Ormond Beach, FL 32176
(904) 441-1808

Located right on Ormond Beach, just a couple of miles north of Daytona Beach, this campground is, perhaps, one of the smallest on Florida's Atlantic coast. It has something of an intimate, even exclusive, atmosphere. The tiny campground is neatly laid out, and the beach features lighted Tiki Huts which give the tiny resort a truly tropical feel.

FACILITIES: There are only 60 available sites, but they all have full-service hookups. Cable TV and telephone hookups are available, too. There's a group site for tents, a very nice, clean bathhouse, sewage disposal, a laundry room, picnic tables and grills. In short, there's just about everything here that you'd expect to find at a much larger campground.

RULES & REGULATIONS: Pets and tenters are welcome.

SECURITY: Good.

NEAREST SERVICES: There's an on-site store where you'll find most of what you need, but you might want to stock up with the more obscure items before you arrive. LP gas is available by weight or meter.

RECREATION: The ocean and the beach are the focus of this campground. Other than that, there's a recreation room and some court games. Fishing, swimming, and boating are popular pastimes and there's a boat ramp for those who bring their own water transportation. There's also a playground for the kids.

NEARBY ATTRACTIONS: Daytona Beach and the International Speedway are just down the road. On the Boardwalk there is a complete entertainment complex featuring amusements, gondola ride, band concerts, and the Space Needle. At Ormond Beach, the Birthplace of Speed Museum (160 East Granada Boulevard), is a must for motor racing enthusiasts. The Casements (25 Riverside Drive), the restored former home of John D. Rockefeller is where you can view a number of interesting exhibits. Farther to the south you find Fort Pierce, where the St. Lucie County Historical Museum on Seaway Drive is a must-see, if only for the fabulous artifacts on display in the Spanish Treasure Fleet Room. The Ponce De Leon Inlet Lighthouse, now a historic monument and museum at Ponce Inlet, has a park with picnic tables and is a nice stop on your tour along the coast. The Space Coast Science Center at Melbourne is also worth a visit (1510 Highlands Avenue).

RATES: Rates are available on request, and, small as the campground is, you'd better make sure you book early.

OPEN: Year round.

HOW TO GET THERE: From the junction of Highways 40 and A1A, drive north on A1A for four miles.

Sunshine Holiday Camper Resort

1701 North US 1, Ormond Beach, FL 32174-2542
(904) 672-3045

This is one of the most developed commercial campgrounds on Florida's Atlantic coast. It is a completely self-contained resort with facilities and recreation opportunities enough to keep you on-site and wanting for nothing. The beaches are just a short distance away.

FACILITIES: All 232 sites are pull-throughs, 191 of them have full-service hookups to 50 amps, cable TV and telephone hookups, and air-conditioning. Most have patios, grills, and tables. There are group sites for tents. The bathhouses are extensive, modern, and are kept extremely clean. The laundry facilities are also clean and up-to-date; sewage disposal is available for overnight guests.

RULES & REGULATIONS: Pets are welcome but should be kept on a leash. Tenters are welcome, too. The quiet time is 10 PM to 7 AM.

SECURITY: Good. Handled by on-site staff around the clock.

NEAREST SERVICES: There's a full-service store on site, and the shops and supermarkets are only minutes away.

RECREATION: Lots to do. There's a large, heated swimming pool with plenty of pool furniture, a recreation hall and fully equipped pavilion, a lake for fishing, mini-golf, court games, and a resident recreation director to help with planned group activities, organized tours, and to ensure that you don't get bored.

NEARBY ATTRACTIONS: At Ormond Beach, the Birthplace of Speed Museum (160 East Granada Boulevard) is a must for motor racing enthusiasts. The Casements (at 25 Riverside Drive), is the one-time home of John D. Rockefeller. At Daytona Beach, just a couple of miles south, the beach is a must see, as is the International Speedway. Other sites to see are the Gamble Place Historic House Museum (1040 Museum Boulevard in Daytona), the Museum of Arts and Sciences (Museum Boulevard), and the Planetarium is at the Museum of Arts and Sciences. The Halifax Historical Museum (252 South Beach Street, Daytona), and the Boardwalk, a complete entertainment complex featuring amusements, gondola ride, band concerts, and the Space Needle are worth your time. You'll find the International Speedway Welcome Center at 1801 West International Speedway Boulevard; tours are available. Farther south lies Fort Pierce and the St. Lucie County Historical Museum (Seaway Drive in Fort Pierce), which has an extensive range of exhibits that include the Spanish Treasure Fleet Room and lots of interesting artifacts recovered from the ocean floor. The Ponce De Leon Inlet Lighthouse, now a historic monument and museum at Ponce Inlet, has a park with picnic tables where you can take time out during your tour along the coast. The Space Coast Science Center at Melbourne is also worth a visit (1510 Highlands Avenue).

RATES: Start at around $20 per night for two persons. This is a very busy campground and reservations should be made well in advance, regardless of season.

OPEN: Year round.

HOW TO GET THERE: From Exit 89 on Interstate 95, take US 1 north for ½ mile.

Titusville Area

Great Outdoors RV Nature & Golf Resort

4505 West Cheney Highway, Titusville, FL 32780
(800) 621-2267

The Great Outdoors is the result of a dream. It was developed by world-famous entrepreneur, philanthropist and environmentalist, Jack Eckerd. "My idea was to make a unique place for people that would also preserve this special environment for nature and wildlife." There's no doubt that Jack Eckerd achieved all he set out to do, for the resort is just as much a wildlife reserve as it is a playground for campers and visitors.

The owners have gone to great lengths to make the resort a very special one. They toured the country, looking at other RV resorts, and they took the best ideas fromeach one. These were incorporated them in the Great Outdoors, all to good purpose, for the resort is one of only four campgrounds in the nation that is consistently 10/10/10 by *Trailer Life*. This is a resort in every sense of the word. The park encompasses more than 2,800 acres – 1,700 of them are still undeveloped and have been set aside as a wildlife preserve where nature can exist in harmony with man.

FACILITIES: There are 750 sites, all large, with landscaped gardens and concrete pads, full-service hookups and underground facilities that include water, electric to 50 amps, sewer, telephone and cable TV. The rest of the facilities are equally extensive: five immaculate bathhouses, laundry room, comfort stations, and rain shelters. There's also a health club, and a hobbyland where you can use woodworking equipment or get involved in arts and crafts. All restrooms, bathhouses, comfort stations, and public buildings are handicapped accessible.

RULES & REGULATIONS: Pets are welcome but must be kept under control at all times. No tents, pop-up trailers, RVs or trailers under 18 feet in length. RVs and trailers must be able to connect to the full-service hookups.

SECURITY: Excellent. Provided by a 24-hour, manned security system with regular patrols throughout the day and night and a guard on the gate at all times.

NEAREST SERVICES: On the property. There's a full-service store where you can buy almost everything you need: groceries, camping supplies, paper goods, and gasoline. There's also a beauty shop, post office, ATM, and a user-exchange library.

RECREATION: While the focus of the park is on its 18-hole championship golf course, there's so much more to see and do. On-site facilities include a 14,000-square-foot recreation center complete with an elevated stage, dance floor, kitchen, and a giant screen for movies and TV. There are two heated swimming pools with plenty of room for relaxing and sunning, and a heated whirlpool. The health club is extensively equipped with modern exercise machines and a sauna. If you're an angler, you'll have access to 16 lakes where you can hunt trophy-size largemouth and sunshine bass, crappie, bluegill, channel catfish, warmouth perch, and shellcracker. The lakes are kept stocked by a full-time wildlife manager. The golf course is one to be envied by even exclusive country clubs. Eighteen challenging holes over one of southern Florida's most picturesque courses can be followed by a multi-course lunch in the clubhouse dining room, or a couple of drinks at the 19th. There's also a driving range, putting green, and a full-service pro shop. Apart from the usual court games, there's also a croquet lawn and two lighted tennis courts. A full-time recreation director is always on hand to take care of your needs and provide a full program of planned group activities.

NEARBY ATTRACTIONS: Walt Disney World, Universal Studios, and EPCOT are less than a hour away. The Kennedy Space Center is only six miles of Indian River (you can see the shuttle blast off from the resort), the Canaveral National Seashore is just to the northeast, Titusville itself is just up the road, and Indian River City is even closer – almost within walking distance. The St. Johns distance. The St. Johns National Wildlife Refuge is close, and Orlando is 26 miles west along Highway 50.

RATES: November through April the rate for two people is $27 daily, $189 weekly, and $575 per month, with each additional month subject to a $50 discount. May through October, $23 per day, $147 per week, $525 for the first month, and $471 for each additional month. Add $3 for each extra person.

OPEN: Year round.

HOW TO GET THERE: From Exit 79 on Interstate 95, drive ½ mile west on Highway 50 (Cheney Highway).

Crystal Lake RV Park

PO Box 362, Scottsmoor, FL 32775-0362.
(407) 268-8555

This a one of the east coast's smaller campgrounds and, though it's rather short on conventional facilities, it's long on aesthetics and outdoor opportunities. Set among swamps, woodlands, and a hundred tiny lakes and rivers to the west of Indian River and the Canaveral National Seashore, it is in a rather remote area, but not so remote that you'll want to bypass it for a more inhabited location. The beaches, dog track, jai alai, and Speedway are all only minutes away. The campground itself is exceptionally well-kept, kind of intimate, and very appealing.

FACILITIES: Of the 65 over-sized sites, 60 have full-service hookups to 30 amps, most have tables, and 60 are pull-throughs. The bathhouse is kept scrupulously clean, and there's always plenty of hot water for the showers. The laundry room is modern and well-equipped; sewage disposal is available and there are public telephones on the property.

RULES & REGULATIONS: Pets are welcome, but should be kept on a leash. Tenters are welcome.

SECURITY: Good. Handled by on-site staff.

NEAREST SERVICES: There's a convenience store at the intersection of Interstate 95 and Stuck Way Road, just a short walk from the campground. There are a couple of restaurants there, too. It would be best if you stocked up on the essentials before you arrive.

RECREATION: There's a recreation hall and a nice swimming pool with room to stretch out and relax. A three-acre lake is kept well-stocked with bass and catfish, and you can rent a canoe for a quiet afternoon of paddling. If you're an angler, all the opportunities provided by the Canaveral National Seashore and Indian River are close at hand. Public access boat ramps are located at Cedar Island, Arial, Apollo Beach, Scottsmoor, Wiley and just off the Max Brewer Memorial Parkway and Veterans Memorial Park Pier in Titusville.

NEARBY ATTRACTIONS: The Kennedy Space Center is about eight miles east of Indian River, and the Canaveral National Seashore is northeast. Daytona Beach and the International Speedway are just to the north along Interstate 95, and Daytona's Boardwalk is a complete entertainment complex with amusements, rides, and band concerts. At Ormond Beach, the Birthplace of Speed Museum (160 East Granada Boulevard), is a must for motor racing enthusiasts. Titusville is just down the road a short distance to the south. The Space Coast Science Center at Melbourne is also worth a visit (1510 Highlands Avenue). Indian River City is just beyond Titusville and to the south you'll find Fort Pierce. Walt Disney World, Universal Studios, and EPCOT are about an hour west. The Ponce De Leon Inlet Lighthouse, now a historic monument and museum, is at Ponce Inlet.

RATES: Start at around $20 per night for two persons.

OPEN: Year round.

HOW TO GET THERE: From Exit 82 on Interstate 95, drive one block east on Stuck Way Road.

Central West Coast

It's here that the manatees join the tourists in their annual pilgrimage to the warm waters of the Gulf of Mexico, to bask in the sunshine and relax as they wait for the warmer weather.

For more than 400 years this area of Florida's west coast has been welcoming visitors. The first to arrive were the Spanish conquistadors. They came in search of gold, which they didn't find. More than 300 years later, another visitor saw the real potential of the area. Henry Plant brought the railroad to Tampa, and it was he that built the onion-domed hotel that was to become a famous local landmark.

The downtown Tampa skyline and harbor.

Then came the Greek sponge fishermen who settled in Tarpon Springs, who still harvest the sponges just as they did almost a century ago. The Greeks were followed by clansmen from the highlands of Scotland; they settled in Dunedin. Next came Cubans who settled in Tampa and created the Hav-a-Tampa cigar industry; their warehouses eventually became trendy gathering places with elegant cafés, artist's studios, fancy ethnic restaurants, and chic specialty shops.

Today, the heart of vacation country on the central west coast encompasses the neighboring cities of Tampa and St. Petersburg, supported to the north by a captivating collection of island communities, such as Indian Rocks Beach, Madeira Beach and Treasure Island. To the south lie Anna Marie Island, Longboat Key, Siesta Key and many more that offer even more interesting opportunities. You can also consider mile after mile of tempting white sand, clear green ocean, and gently waving tropical trees.

Bradenton

Pleasant Lake RV Resort

6633 53rd Avenue East, Bradenton, FL 34203
(800) 283-5076

With its own 25-acre bass fishing lake, and situated close to the Braden and Manatee Rivers, Tampa Bay, Sarasota Bay, and the beaches, this urban resort, with its extensive range of facilities and services, qualifies as one of the best of its type in the Bradenton area. It's also the largest camping resort here. Extremely well-planned and laid out, the campsites encircle a large lake and all are within easy reach of the facilities.

FACILITIES: Of the 670 sites, all have full-service hookups to 50 amps, cable TV, and telephone; 56 are pull-throughs. There are two modern, well-kept, handicapped accessible, bathhouses, two laundry rooms, sewage disposal facilities, and each site has a patio.

RULES & REGULATIONS: Pets are allowed but must not weigh over 25 pounds. They must be kept on a leash while on the property. The quiet time is 10 PM to 7 AM.

SECURITY: Excellent. The property is gated and there's a guard on duty. The gate is locked at night and you must a have gate card to enter.

NEAREST SERVICES: There's a new shopping plaza across the street with a Publix Supermarket, two banks, a dry cleaner and several restaurants. LP gas is available on the property by weight or meter.

RECREATION: There are two recreation areas on the property, one on either side of the lake. Both have court games, and the one on the west side of the campground has a recreation hall, a heated pool with a patio, and a whirlpool. The lake is well stocked with bass and you can fish from the shore or boat. There's a boat ramp and dock, 10 shuffleboard courts, several basketball hoops, and a recreation director who takes care of a winter program of planned group activities. The beaches are a few miles east, the shopping center in Bradenton is even closer, and Tampa/St. Petersburg is north via Interstate 75.

NEARBY ATTRACTIONS: With all that's available in the immediate vicinity of the campground, you'll find yourself a little overwhelmed. Try to visit the Manatee Village Historical Park on 15th Street East in Bradenton. It's on the National Register of Historic Places and contains five buildings of historic interest (admission free; 813-749-7165). The South Florida Museum and Bishop Planetarium is also worth a visit (210 West 10th St., Bradenton; admission $5; 813-746-4131). The Gamble Plantation State Historic Site (3708 Patten Avenue in Ellenton), across the Manatee River from Bradenton, is a historic ante-bellum mansion that was once the heart of thriving sugar industry (admission $5; 813-723-4536). Gator Jungle is the place to go if you want to see Florida's monsters.

RATES: Standard sites are $25 per night for two persons; lakeview and corner sites are $28.

OPEN: Year round.

HOW TO GET THERE: From Exit 41 on Interstate 75, drive west for ½ mile on Highway 70.

Horseshoe Cove RV Resort

5100 60th Street, Bradenton, FL 34203
(800) 291-3446

Though not on the beach, this is one of the most popular RV resorts in the Tampa/St. Petersburg area. The facilities are extensive, both for camping and recreation. Set on the banks of the Braden River, and surrounded by landscaped grounds and woodland.

FACILITIES: Of the 477 sites, all are paved, have full-service hookups to 50 amps, telephone hookups, and concrete patios. The paved roads are wide and there are plenty of places to turn a large RV around. The restrooms and some of the facilities are handicapped accessible, and there's hot water for the showers around the clock. The laundry rooms are modern, well-equipped and maintained, sewage disposal is available for overnight campers, and there are public telephones handy to most sites.

RULES & REGULATIONS: No tents, trailers or pop-ups: self-contained RVs only. Pets are welcome but must be kept on a leash.

SECURITY: Excellent. The campground is on a private island, gated, and there's a guard on duty.

NEAREST SERVICES: Groceries are available, adjacent to the island. There are two outlet centers less than 10 minutes away, and there are supermarkets in Bradenton.

RECREATION: The resort is unique for its music program: you can take guitar lessons, attend band concerts, chorus recitals, and Broadway-type musicals. Also on the property you'll have access to a 1.3-mile fitness course, a large heated swimming pool with plenty of furniture and room to relax, a woodworking shop where you can take instruction and make all sorts of small crafts, tennis courts, court games, and a recreation direction who will look after most of your needs and provide a program of planned group activities during the winter months.

NEARBY ATTRACTIONS: Most of the local action and attractions are to the west in St. Petersburg, Clearwater and Tampa. The big attractions in the Orlando area – Walt Disney World, Sea World, Universal Studios, etc., are less than an hour to the east via Inter-

Interstate 4. For more ideas you can check the oth.
section.

RATES: Start at around $32 per night for two persons. Call
details.

OPEN: Year round.

HOW TO GET THERE: From Exit 41 on Interstate 75, drive 1.2
miles west on Highway 70, then ¼ mile north on Caruso Road.

Cedar Key

Cedar Key RV Park

PO Box 268, Cedar Key, FL 32625-0268
(904) 543-5150

This tiny campground is included in this book mainly because of
its location. If you're looking for peace and quiet, a great place to
go fishing, or for spectacular natural beauty, this is it. This is not the
place to go if you're looking for luxury, nightlife, and action. Facilities are limited, but what it lacks in amenities it makes up for in
aesthetics.

FACILITIES: There are only 29 sites, all with full-service hookups
to 30 amps, and tables. The bathhouse has flush toilets and hot
showers.

RULES & REGULATIONS: Pets are welcome if kept on a leash.
Tenters are also welcome.

SECURITY: Good. Handled by on-site staff.

NEAREST SERVICES: Cedar Key is within walking distance.

RECREATION: Fishing (there's a private fishing pier on the property), walking, relaxing, sketching, painting, and photography. The
scenery is spectacular.

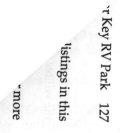

r Key RV Park   127

listings in this

more

t for two persons. Very popular during
o book early.

ke Highway 24 to Cedar Key. From the
rn north and drive ½ mile on Whiden
G Street.

Dunedin

Dunedin Beach Campground

2920 Alt 19 N. Dunedin, FL 34698
(800) 831-0550

Dunedin Beach is one of those idyllic spots on the Gulf Coast one often sees in commercials but rarely can find – the sands are pristine and white, the waters of the Gulf a pale emerald green, and the weather always seems to be balmy. The campground, surrounded by woodland and marshes, is just as appealing.

FACILITIES: Of the 233 sites, all have full-service hookups to 30 amps, telephone hookups, and picnic tables. The bathhouses are clean and modern, and there's always plenty of hot water for the showers. There's a modern, well-equipped laundry room; sewage disposal is available for overnight campers, and there are public telephones close to most sites.

RULES & REGULATIONS: Pets are welcome but must be kept on a leash. Tenters are welcome, too. The quiet time is 10 PM to 7 AM.

SECURITY: Very good. Handled by on-site staff.

NEAREST SERVICES: There's a store on the property where you can buy some of what you need, including a limited range of groceries, paper goods, and gifts. The shops, however, are less than a half-mile away. LP gas is available on the property by weight or meter.

RECREATION: There's a nice recreation hall with coin operated games, a large heated swimming pool with lots of furniture and plenty of room to relax, a playground for the kids, and a resident recreation director to look after your needs, answer questions, book shows and tours, and provide planned group activities during the winter months. For hikers, there are trails through the surrounding woods and marshes, the beaches are close at hand and provide more opportunities for walking, as well as shelling, beachcombing, swimming, fishing, and sunning. The sunsets are often spectacular. The causeway to Honeymoon Island State Park, one of the few totally unspoiled off-shore islands in the area, is just a half-mile away.

NEARBY ATTRACTIONS: Clearwater and St. Petersburg are south, Tampa is southeast, and Walt Disney World and Orlando are an hour east via Interstate 4. Locally, you might like to visit Adventure Island, a 22-acre outdoor water theme park (10 AM-5 PM; admission, $15; 4500 East Bougainvillea Ave., Tampa, 813-987-5660) or you could try a balloon flight over the Tampa area offered by Big Red Balloon Fantasy Flights (call for rates; 16302 East Course Drive, Tampa; 813-969-4381). Busch Gardens, also in Tampa, is a world famous, 300-acre African-themed family entertainment park offering a variety of rides, shows, shops and restaurants (9:30 AM-6 PM; admission, $20; 3000 East Busch Blvd.; 813-987-5082). In Clearwater you might like to visit the Marine Science Center Aquarium (249 Windward Passage, 9AM-5PM; admission, $5; 813-441-1790). In St. Petersburg there's a unique experience to be had at Great Explorations, The Hands-On Museum (1120 Fourth St. South; 10AM-5PM; admission $5; 813-821-8885).

RATES: The rate starts at around $21 for two persons per night.

OPEN: Year round.

HOW TO GET THERE: From the junction of Highways 586 and Alt 19N., drive ¾ mile north on Alt 19.

Jennings

Jennings Outdoor Resort

I-75 & State Road 143, Exit 87, Jennings, FL 32053
(904) 938-3321

The first conveniently located commercial campground as you travel south out of Georgia into Florida is this one on Interstate 75. Its extensive range of facilities make it a great place to stop on your way to the resorts farther south. Not a large campground by Florida standards, but it is well equipped to service most needs. It's well planned, clean, with a courteous, helpful staff on hand to answer any travel questions you may have.

FACILITIES: Of the 102 available sites, all have patios, full-service hookups to 50 amps, and all are pull-throughs. Roads and pads are all paved, the bathhouse is in top condition; there's plenty of hot water for the showers, the laundry room is modern, and cable TV is available for a charge. Tents can be rented.

RULES & REGULATIONS: Pets are welcome so long as they are kept under control. Tenters are welcome.

SECURITY: Very good. Handled by on-site staff.

NEAREST SERVICES: There's a full-service store on the property where you can buy groceries, paper goods, and most other essentials, as well as gasoline and LP gas by weight or meter. There are a number of fast-food restaurants close by.

RECREATION: There's a nice recreation hall, a heated swimming pool with plenty of room for sunbathing, a playground for the kids, lots of court games, and a nearby lake where you can fish or boat. Rental canoes and pedal boats can be rented on the property.

RATES: Start at around $15 per night for two persons. Specials for senior citizens. At the time of writing, the first night free was offered with a minimum stay of three nights. Check to make sure.

OPEN: Year round.

HOW TO GET THERE: From Exit 87 on Interstate 75, drive 500 feet west on Highway 143.

Leesburg

Lake Griffin State Recreation Area

103 Highway 441/27, Fruitland Park, FL 34731
(904) 787-7402

Along with its superb bass fishing, Lake Griffin, less than an hour from Florida's major commercial attractions, strives to offer something for the whole family. It's an outdoor attraction that compares favorably with any of Florida's other parks. The countryside is breath-taking, the lake beautiful, and the sunsets are often spectacular. The facilities, though somewhat limited, are clean and well-maintained, and opportunities for outdoor recreation abound.

FACILITIES: There are 40 full-service campsites, all with water and electric hookups, picnic tables and grills. The restrooms and bathhouse are handicapped accessible, with flush toilets and hot showers. There are public telephones on the property.

RULES & REGULATIONS: No pets, but guide dogs are welcome. Alcohol and firearms prohibited. Do not feed wild animals.

SECURITY: Very good. Round-the-clock security by a resident park manager. The gates are locked from sunset to 8 AM. Campers are provided with the combination to the gate lock, allowing free exit and access after the park has closed.

NEAREST SERVICES: The nearest full-service grocery store is less then two miles away in Leesburg, and there are convenience stores close at hand.

RECREATION: Hiking, boating, canoeing, swimming, and picnicking are all popular activities, but the Lake Griffin area is famous for great fishing. Many thousands of acres of water, on a number of large lakes, all interlinked by rivers and creeks, offer endless opportunities for sport, and all are heavily stocked with largemouth, smallmouth, striped and sunshine bass, bream, speck-led perch, shellcracker, warmouth, stumpknocker, redbreast, sun-fish, and catfish. There's a boat ramp on the property, and at least a dozen more within easy driving distance (say 30 minutes). There's also a concession stand where you can buy fishing supplies, gifts, food and drink, and rent canoes. If you're a golfer, there a nice 18-hole course just four miles to the north at Lady Lake.

RATES: May through October, $8 per night. November through April, $10 per night.

OPEN: Year round.

HOW TO GET THERE: From Leesburg, take Highway 441/27 and drive north for two miles.

Live Oak

Spirit Of Suwannee

Box 98, Live Oak, FL 32060
(904) 364-1683

When compiling our list of campgrounds we were aware of the need to provide something extra, campgrounds with a difference, and that's just what we have here. The emphasis is on music of all kinds, not just down-home country music. True, you'll often find big-name country stars in attendance, but you're just as likely to hear a retired steel worker from Pennsylvania singing about life on the farm, or a Canadian playing haunting tunes of the Old West on a harmonica. Maybe you'll hear the sounds of children singing the happy tunes of childhood, or you might even hear the old gospel songs sung with such emotion and feeling it'll make your hair stand on end. The Spirit of Suwannee is not a place to stand and watch, at least not all the time. You might be asked to help with the stage, build a float, get involved, but most of all to enjoy yourself. If it's a different type of camping experience you're looking for, you'll certainly find it at the Spirit of Suwannee. The 600-acre park/campground is bordered to the north by the Suwannee, an incredibly beautiful river that gently winds southward from the

Okefenokee Swamp to the Gulf of Mexico. The river bank is bordered by live oaks, cypress trees, Spanish moss, interlaced with woodland trails that often echo with the faint sounds of music from the park.

FACILITIES: Of the 150 sites, 97 have full-service hookups and 90 are pull-throughs. Camping trailers and tents are available for rent. There's a well-equipped laundry room, The bathhouses are clean and roomy, and sewage disposal is available for overnight campers.

RULES & REGULATIONS: Pets are welcome but must be kept on a leash.

SECURITY: Good. 24-hours by on-site staff.

NEAREST SERVICES: There's a mini-mart just outside the gate where you can buy the essentials, and there are supermarkets about four miles away in Live Oak.

RECREATION: The focus here is on the the music and live entertainment. There's an indoor theater and an outdoor amphitheater where big-name groups perform everything from country to bluegrass, and from old-time, farm music to gospel. Other than that, the Suwannee River, the woodlands and forests, provide all sorts of outdoor opportunities for hiking, fishing, boating, canoeing, or just strolling on the riverbank. On-site, you can swim in the pool, rent canoes, and take part in the program of planned group activities. Then there are court games, a playground, picnic tables, etc.

NEARBY ATTRACTIONS: Almost everything of interest here revolves around the Suwannee River and its heritage. The Suwannee River State Park is just to the north and Falmouth Springs to the south. The Stephen Foster Memorial State Park is at White Springs where you'll find the historic Telford Hotel, headquarters of For The People Network, and from which Chuck Harder broadcasts on weekdays. You can visit, watch the show and eat lunch, if you like. The Osceola National Forest and Olustee Battlefield State Historic Site are a few miles east. Jacksonville is about 120 miles east and Tallahassee about the same distance west.

RATES: Very reasonable at $15 per night for two to four people: AARP and NCHA discounts are honored, too.

OPEN: Year round.

HOW TO GET THERE: From the junction Interstate 75 and Highway 129, drive south on 129 for four miles.

Suwannee River State Park

Route 8, Box 297, Live Oak, FL 32060
(904) 362-2764

Here, where the scenic Withlacoochee River joins the Suwannee River, naturalists and lovers of the outdoors will find a great deal to enjoy. The park encompasses more than 1,800 acres of wild and natural habitat from sandhill to river swamp, and includes many diverse plant communities. On a good day, nature watchers might catch a glimpse of the great horned owl, wild turkeys, red tailed hawks, otters, gopher turtles, woodpeckers, beavers, and, of course, alligators. Also of interest are the earthworks built during the Civil War by Confederate soldiers to protect the railroad bridge across the Suwannee, an important link in the supply line that took beef, salt, sugar, and other essential supplies to the Confederate armies fighting in Virginia, Tennessee, and Georgia. Of interest, too, is the cemetery and the landing that once serviced the river boats as they carried goods and passengers back and forth along the river. While the park is quite large, the campground is small and intimate, but it does provide lots of opportunities for outdoor living and recreation.

FACILITIES: All 31 sites have water and electric hookups, table, and grills. The restrooms are handicapped accessible, and the bathhouse has flush toilets and hot showers. There's a youth camping facility for use by non-profit groups.

RULES & REGULATIONS: No pets, but guide dogs are welcome. Alcohol and firearms prohibited. Do not feed wild animals.

SECURITY: Very good. Round-the-clock security by a resident park manager. The gates are locked from sunset to 8 AM. Campers are provided with the combination to the gate lock, allowing free exit and access after the park has closed.

NEAREST SERVICES: The nearest full-service supermarkets are either 13 miles east along Highway 90 in Live Oak, or 14 miles west in Madison, also on Highway 90. Be sure to stock up before you arrive.

RECREATION: The emphasize here is on the river and the great outdoors. There are a number of nature and hiking trails on the property, as well as a boat ramp which provides access to the river. There's also a picnic area with two covered pavilions. Activities you might enjoy include bird watching (especially on the Suwannee River Trail), wildlife photography, fishing, and canoeing. For canoeists, there are a number of excellent opportunities, including the Upper Suwannee River Canoe Trail and the Withlacoochee River Canoe Trail, both of which begin in Georgia and end in the park. The Lower Suwannee River Canoe Trail begins in the park and ends in the Gulf of Mexico. For fishermen, there are catfish, largemouth bass, redbreast sunfish, and other panfish to hunt.

RATES: October through February, $8 per night. March through September, $10 per night.

OPEN: Year round.

HOW TO GET THERE: The park is located 13 miles to the northwest of Live Oak, off Highway 90.

Tampa & St. Petersburg

Hillsborough River State Park

15402 U.S Highway 301 North, Thonotosassa, FL 33592
(813) 986-1020

Hillsborough River is one of Florida's first state parks. It was developed by the Civilian Conservation Corps in 1936 and opened to the general public two years later. Of special interest is Fort Foster, a pioneer fort located within the park, where Park service personnel run programs of living history, acting out the everyday lives and duties of the early settlers, as they might have been in 1837. The campground is exceptionally nice, not large by Florida standards, but well served with facilities and opportunities for recreation. The park itself encompasses more than 2,900 acres of hammock and forest with stands of live oak, hickory, sabal palm, and magnolias that border the Hillsborough River.

FACILITIES: All 118 sites in two separate areas have water and electric hookups, picnic tables, and grills. The restrooms have flush toilets, hot showers, and all facilities are handicapped accessible. There's a youth campsite for use by non-profit organizations. Facilities available for those hardy types who enjoy primitive camping.

RULES & REGULATIONS: No pets, but guide dogs are welcome. Alcohol and firearms prohibited. Do not feed wild animals.

SECURITY: Very good. Round-the-clock security by a resident park manager. The gates are locked from sunset to 8 AM. Campers are provided with the combination to the gate lock, allowing free exit and access after the park has closed.

NEAREST SERVICES: There's a concession stand on the property where you can buy some supplies: food and drink, gifts, fishing tackle, etc., but the nearest supermarket is about six miles away in Zephyrhills. It might be wise to stock up with what you need before you arrive.

RECREATION: For hikers, there are more than eight miles of nature trails that wind through the park and along the banks of the river. Anglers will enjoy the fine sport provided by the Hillsborough River: bass, bream, shellcracker, and catfish. There's a swimming pool on the property, and you can go canoeing or boating on the river; canoes may be rented at the concession stand.

RATES: $13 per night.

OPEN: Year round.

HOW TO GET THERE: The park is located 12 miles north of Tampa or six miles south of Zephyrhills on Highway 301.

Tampa E. Green Acres Camp/RV Park

4630 McIntosh Road, Dover, FL 33527
(813) 659-0002

This is actually a two-park facility with less than ¼ mile between units, both handily situated on Interstate 4, and within easy reach of the beaches.

FACILITIES: There are 580 extra-large sites, of which 564 have full-service hookups, telephone hookups, picnic tables, and 120 are pull-throughs. The bathhouse are clean, handy, and there's hot water around the clock for the showers. The restrooms and some other facilities are handicapped accessible. Sewage disposal is available for overnight campers. There are laundry facilities at both locations and public telephones are handy to all sites.

RULES & REGULATIONS: Pets are welcome. Tenters are welcome. Quiet time between 10 PM and 7 AM.

SECURITY: Good. Handled by resident staff.

In downtown Tampa the Florida Aquarium focuses exclusively on Florida's waterlife.

NEAREST SERVICES: There are convenience stores at both campgrounds which supply a limited range of groceries, paper goods, etc. The nearest major supermarket is not far away in Plant City. LP gas is available on the property by weight or meter. McDonald's is right next door.

RECREATION: There's a large recreation hall (it seats 300). At each campground there's a heated swimming pool with lots of furniture and a patio. There are several ponds where you can go fishing. There's a playground for the children, and all the usual court games are available, including horseshoes and shuffleboard. There's an 18-hole golf course nearby. The beaches at Clearwater and St. Petersburg are only minutes away down Interstate 4 and all the attractions of the Orlando area (Walt Disney World, Sea World, Universal Studios, etc.) are 50 minutes east, also along Interstate 4.

NEARBY ATTRACTIONS: Tampa, St. Petersburg, Clearwater and Dunedin are just 12 miles east on Interstate 4. Six miles west lies Plant City, where you can visit Gator Jungle, a farm dedicated to the study and preservation of Florida's most famous resident (8:30AM-6PM; admission less than $10; I-4 and Branch Forbes, Plant City, 813-752-2836). The Lowery Park Zoo (7530 North Boulevard, Tampa), a must-visit, is one of the three largest zoos in North America (9:30AM-5PM; less than $10; 813-935-8552). You also might like to try the Museum of Fine Arts (at 255 Beach Drive, St. Petersburg; 10AM-5PM; less than $5; 813-896-2667).

No visit to the Tampa/St. Petersburg area would be complete without a visit to The Pier in St. Petersburg. The great, five-story inverted pyramid dominates the skyline and seascape. Inside there are lots of shops, bars, grills, an aquarium, and an observation deck (800 Second Avenue; open year-round; free; 813-821-6164).

RATES: Start at around $22 for two persons per night.

OPEN: Year round.

HOW TO GET THERE: From Exit 9 on Interstate 4, drive ¼ mile south on McIntosh Road, then ¼ mile west on Highway 92.

Palm Harbor

Clearwater Tarpon Springs KOA

12870 Hwy. 92, Dover, FL 33527
(813) 659-2202

For something different, you might like to give this, secluded campground a try. It's not on the beach, but it is close to the water

FACILITIES: There are 118 large, landscaped sites, of which 80 have full-service hookups to 30 amps. Cable TV is available. There are a half-dozen Kamping Kabins available. The restrooms and some of the other facilities are handicapped accessible. The bathhouse is clean, the laundry facilities modern and well-maintained, and most of the sites have tables and patios.

RULES & REGULATIONS: Pets are welcome, but must be kept under control at all times. Tenters are welcome. The quiet time is 10 PM until 7 AM.

SECURITY: Good. Handled by resident staff.

NEAREST SERVICES: There's a nice store on the property where you can find most of what you need, and there are supermarkets nearby. There are also a number of very nice restaurants within driving distance of the campground.

RECREATION: There's a large recreation hall, a pavilion with coin-operated games, a heated swimming pool with lots of furniture and plenty of room to relax, a playground, and a covered picnic shelter with tables and grills. If you like to fish, you'll find Lake Tarpon will suit your needs admirably (largemouth and sunshine bass, bream and shellcracker abound). If it's a more exciting sport you're after, you can charter a deep-sea fishing boat nearby and head out on to the Gulf of Mexico.

NEARBY ATTRACTIONS: All the attractions listed for other campgrounds in the immediate area are close at hand. The major attractions at Orlando are 50 minutes away along Interstate 4, Clearwater is less than six miles south. St. Petersburg is a little farther south and Tampa is southeast. The beaches are a few minutes west. Check other listings for specific attractions.

RATES: A basic tent site without hookups is $15.50 per night for two persons. A full-service site is $29.95. A one-room Kamping Kabin is $37.50. Extra persons are charged $3 extra per night.

OPEN: Year round.

HOW TO GET THERE: From the junction of Highways 584 and 19, drive two miles north on Highway 19.

Sarasota

Myakka River State Park

13207 S.R. 72, Sarasota, FL 34241
(813) 361-6511

Myakka River is one of the largest parks in the Florida system, covering an area of 28,875 acres. It is a vast, diverse land of wild and scenic beauty featuring natural plant communities, lakes, river marshes, hammocks, and prairies.

The Myakka River flows for more than 12 miles through the park on its journey to the Gulf of Mexico. The main road winds through oak and palm hammocks, grassy mashes, sloughs, and the Upper Myakka Lake. Deer, raccoon, and many species of wild birds can be observed, either from the park drive, or from the wooden bird walk.

Across the large, open expanses of pine flatwoods, prairies, and wetlands, cottontails, red-shouldered hawks, deer, and bobcats can be seen at home in their natural environment. If you love the great outdoors, you'll find that Myakka River truly is a naturalist's paradise.

FACILITIES: In keeping with the size of the park, the facilities at Myakka River are varied and extensive, ranging from full-service to tent campsites to rustic rental cabins furnished with two beds and a sofa-bed. There's a boat basin and dock located on the Upper Myakka Lake. There's also a concession facility on the Upper Myakka Lake where you can rent boats, canoes, and bicycles, or purchase camping, picnicking, and fishing supplies, along with snacks, soft drinks, and souvenirs.

RULES & REGULATIONS: No pets, but guide dogs are welcome. Alcohol and firearms prohibited. Do not feed wild animals.

SECURITY: Excellent. Round-the-clock security by a resident park manager. The gates are locked from sunset to 8 AM. Campers are provided with the combination to the gate lock, allowing free exit and access after the park has closed.

NEAREST SERVICES: The nearest supermarket is 12 miles away in Sarasota, so it would be a good idea to stock up on the essentials before you arrive.

RECREATION: Backpacking the many miles of wetland and woodland trails through the hammock, prairies, and pine flatwoods is a popular pastime. Horseback riding along more than 15 miles of bridleways is available to visitors with their own horses. Fishing the Myakka River and Upper Myakka Lake is excellent (largemouth and smallmouth bass, bluegill, crappie, bream, and catfish). Canoeing on the river and lake and bird watching and wildlife photography are other possibilities.

NEARBY ATTRACTIONS: Sarasota Jungle Gardens is at 3701 Bay Shore Gardens, the National Police Museum is in North Port, Lover's Key State Recreation Area is between Fort Myers Beach and Bonita Beach in Lee County, the Everglades Wonder Gardens are in Bonita Springs, and the City of Fort Myers is south. You might also like to visit the Sanibel Lighthouse on Sanibel Island, Port Charlotte Beach near Englewood, the Circus Winter Quarters at Venice, the Fakahatchee Strand State Preserve south of Naples, and the Thomas Edison and Ford Winter Homes at Fort Myers.

RATES: Campsites are $12 per night October 1 through February 28, and $17 per night March 1 through September 30. Call for cabin rates.

OPEN: Year round.

HOW TO GET THERE: The park is 12 miles east of Sarasota on SR 72.

Oscar Scherer State Recreation Area

1843 S. Tamiami Trail, Osprey, FL 34229
(813) 483-5956

Oscar Scherer State Recreation Area is an extensive tract of scrubby and pine flatwoods. The scrubby flatwoods offer a natural and protected habitat to Florida's diminishing population of rare and endangered birds and animals, including the Florida scrub jay, the gopher tortoise, the gopher frog, and the indigo snake. Bald eagles, bobcats, river otters, and alligators also can often be seen in the park during the winter months.

The pine flatwoods, the second major plant community in the park, offers a home to a wide variety of songbirds and woodpeckers, as well as the occasional gopher tortoise.

FACILITIES: The camping area has all the usual facilities, including 104 sites, all with water and electric hookups and picnic tables. The bathhouse and restrooms are handicapped accessible, have flush toilets, and hot showers. There's also a primitive camping area for those who want to get close to nature. There are campfire circles, and canoes may be rented by the hour or by the day at the ranger station.

RULES & REGULATIONS: No pets, but guide dogs are welcome. Alcohol and firearms prohibited. Do not feed wild animals.

SECURITY: Excellent. Round-the-clock security by a resident park manager. The gates are locked from sunset to 8 AM. Campers are provided with the combination to the gate lock, allowing free exit and access after the park has closed.

NEAREST SERVICES: Just minutes away on Highway 41.

RECREATION: While the park is an important destination for naturalists, bird watchers, and wildlife photographers, it also offers a wide variety of other recreational activities. Camping, canoeing, swimming, and fishing are all popular. Anglers will find the combination of freshwater fishing above the dam, and saltwater fishing below it, a rare and unusual treat, while the small, freshwater Lake Osprey provides a perfect spot for swimming and relaxation.

NEARBY ATTRACTIONS: There's so much to see and do in this area it's difficult to know what to include and what to leave out. Myakka River State Park is just a few miles east off Highway 72, Cayo Costa State Park is in Boca Grande, and the National Police Museum is in North Port. There's Gasparilla Island and the Cape Haze Aquatic Preserve, the city of Fort Myers, Lover's Key State Recreation Area, the Everglades Wonder Gardens at Bonita Springs, Sanibel Island, Port Charlotte Beach near Englewood, Delnor-Wiggins Pass State Recreation Area, the Circus Winter Quarters at Venice, Don Pedro Island State Recreation Area, Collier-Seminole State Park just south of Naples, Fakahatchee Strand

State Preserve, also south of Naples, and the Thomas Edison and Ford Winter Homes at Fort Myers.

RATES: $12 per night October 1 through February 28, $17 per night March 1 through September 30.

OPEN: Year round.

HOW TO GET THERE: The recreation area is on US Highway 41, two miles south of Osprey.

Central Florida

It's here that you'll find the nation's number one tourist attraction, and a few more that are almost as popular. The three great theme parks – Walt Disney World, Sea World, and Universal Studios – draw more visitors to central Florida than all other attractions combined.

Orlando, where you'll find a great many of the area's attractions, is the center of this exciting world. Kissimmee and St. Cloud just to the south represent Florida's equestrian heritage. Ocala, to the north, is where you'll Florida's great flatlands and the Ocala National Forest, a vast wildlife refuge and the largest sandpine forest in the world. In Lake County, you can taste the best of the state's wine industry at one of the many vineyards, or spend a quiet hour or two horseback riding through some of Florida's most scenic countryside. Farther south, the roar of racing engines can be heard for miles around the famous Sebring Motor Racing Circuit. For the outdoor sportsman opportunities abound – there are more than 100 golf courses in the area, 21 tennis centers with 800 courts, and literally hundreds of lakes, rivers, and creeks that offer the finest freshwater fishing in the nation. In Lake County you can fish for world-class bass, and many other freshwater species.

Fort McCoy

Ocklawaha Canoe Outpost RV Park

15260 NE 152nd Place, Fort McCoy, FL 32134-9733
(904) 236-4606

In our efforts to provide new and exciting experiences, we think we've found something that's really different. With so much of the Florida that Ponce De Leon found now gone, one has to wonder what it must have been like when he first set foot ashore. Fortunately, there are one or two areas where the Florida of long ago still exists. The middle portion of the Ocklawaha River is one of them. The 110-mile river originates near the center of the state, flows northward along the edge of the Ocala National Forest, and eventually joins with the St. Johns River south of Palatka. Much of the river remains in the pristine condition of 100 years ago. Today it's an area of great natural beauty. There are no restaurants, motels, gas pumps, waterfront homes or marinas to mar the beauty of the river and the forest. The unpolluted waters of the Ocklawaha flow gently through sub-tropical forests and moss-draped trees. In the early mornings, as the mist rises over the water, the swamps and a hundred narrow waterways are disturbed only by the silent paddles of canoeists as they make their way slowly through the stands of old-growth cypress, swamp maples, and sable palms. High above the waters, the great canopy of the forest provides a natural habitat for more than 200 varieties of wild birds. The forest is home for the bobcat, deer, black bear, and more than 300 other mammals and the waters of the river contain more than 100 species of fish. It can all be enjoyed by canoe. The campground is a small one by Florida standards, and the facilities are somewhat limited, but what it lacks in amenities it more than makes up for in outstanding opportunities for recreation.

FACILITIES: The campground has a range of sites, from the very primitive without hookups or services, to some that border on the luxurious with full-service hookups that include water, sewer, and electricity. The bathhouse is spacious and clean with flush toilets and hot showers. The laundry room is well-maintained and has up-to-date machines.

RULES & REGULATIONS: Pets are welcome, but must be kept under control at all times. Absolutely no firearms are permitted. The quiet time is 10 PM to 7 AM.

SECURITY: Good. Provided by on-site staff.

NEAREST SERVICES: There's a full-service store on the property. Most of the essentials, including beer, snacks, camping and canoeing supplies, fishing tackle and other outdoor related items are available. The nearest grocery store is in Fort McCoy.

RECREATION: Obviously, the focus here is on the forest and the river and the countless small tributaries and narrow waterways. The campground is actually an adventure outpost where the staff takes urban explorers deep into the forests by canoe. Everything you'll need is provided, for a short, three-hour trip or an overnight excursion: canoe, tent and instructions, camping stove, lantern, eating utensils, sleeping bags and pads, woodland tools, water container, ice chest, and life jackets. Once on the river, you'll leave civilization far behind. After checking in, you and your camping gear will be transported about 20 miles to the wayside park. From there you can paddle up the Silver River to Silver Springs, which takes about three hours, or you can head out into the unknown for a few days. Prices for canoe trips range from $12.50 per person, two to a canoe, for a short half-day excursion to $57 for an overnighter.

NEARBY ATTRACTIONS: This is a remote area of Florida and there's not much to see other than the Ocala National Forest, which is all around you. If you don't mind traveling, all the attractions in and around Orlando – Walt Disney World, Sea World and Universal Studios – are 75 miles to the south. Daytona Beach is about the same distance east, Gainesville and Jacksonville are north, and Ocala is 25 miles southwest. All offer a variety of attractions, historical sites and sightseeing opportunities.

RATES: Two persons, $12 per night for a site with full-hookups. $8.50 per night for a primitive tent site.

OPEN: Year round.

HOW TO GET THERE: From the junction of Highways 40 and CR 315, drive north for 11 miles to CR 316. From there, drive east for four miles.

Kissimmee

Kissimmee/Orlando KOA

4771 West Bronson Highway, Kissimmee, FL 34746-7813.
(800) 331-1453

Near Kissimmee, one of Florida's nicest little towns, just south of
Orlando and Walt Disney World, this is a large campground with
a lot to offer. As almost all KOAs are, this one is well-managed,
nicely laid out, and kept scrupulously clean. The sites are large and
paved, and the woodland setting is pleasant and relaxing.

FACILITIES: There are 343 sites, of which 226 have full-service
hookups to 30 amps. The rest have water and electric hookups,
some have picnic tables, and 206 are pull-throughs. In addition,
there are 33 one- and two-room, air-conditioned Kamping Kabins
available for campers who like a roof overhead. The bathhouses are
spacious, very clean and maintained, and there's always plenty of
hot water for the showers. The laundry facilities are also spacious,
with an abundance of modern, clean, and well-maintained
machines. Sewage disposal is available for overnight guests, and
public telephones are handy to all sites.

RULES & REGULATIONS: Pets are welcome. Tenters are
welcome. The quiet time is 10 PM to 7 AM.

SECURITY: Excellent. The campground is gated with a guard on
duty 24 hours, and there's a full staff on hand.

NEAREST SERVICES: There's a full-service store on the property
where you'll find almost everything you might need. Several
supermarkets are just down the road in Kissimmee.

RECREATION: There's a large recreation room, a pavilion with
coin-operated games; a large, L-shaped, heated pool with lots of
pool furniture and plenty of room to relax. There are two children's
pools and a playground. All the usual court games are available,
including tennis and badminton. During the winter months, you
can participate in a full program of planned group activities
supervised by a resident recreation director. You can take a guided tour,

and rental cars are available right on the property. If you like to fish, Lakes Tohopekaliga and East Tohopekaliga are less than six miles away. Both have public access boat ramps and are well-stocked with largemouth bass, crappie, shellcracker and channel catfish. For the golfer, the Airport Inn Golf Club is south of Kissimmee, and the Buenaventura Lakes West Country Club is east of the city.

NEARBY ATTRACTIONS: The campground is the closest KOA to Walt Disney World, Universal Studios, Epcot, and Sea World. Orlando is less than 15 miles north via Interstate 4, the east coast is 35 miles away via Highways 417 and 528, and the west coast (Tampa and St. Petersburg) are less than an hour away via Interstate 4. You might like to visit A World of Orchids (2501 Old Lake Wilson Road, Kissimmee (10AM-6PM; less than $5; 407-396-1887). Alligatorland Safari Zoo (4580 W Highway 92, Kissimmee; 8:30AM-6PM; less than $5; 407-396-1012) is where you can see more than 200 alligators. Bok Tower Gardens are in Lake Wales (8AM-5PM; less than $5; 813-676-6770), and Church Street Station (129 West Church), is Orlando's downtown center for dining and shopping. If you'd like to experience the thrills of a high speed flight you could try Fighter Pilots USA for a flight of air combat maneuvering at speeds in excess of 250 miles an hour (3033 W Patrick St., Kissimmee; 407-931-4333). You could also go for a balloon flight with Central Florida Balloon Tours, Winter Park (around $25; 407-294-8085).

RATES: Start at $17.95 per night for a basic tent site for two persons. A site with full-service hookups is $29.95. A one-room Kabin is $38 per night, and a two-room Kabin is $44 per night. Extra persons are charged $4 per night.

OPEN: Year round.

HOW TO GET THERE: From the junction of Interstate 4 and Highway 192, drive east on 192 for 4½ miles.

Tropical Palms Resort

2650 Holiday Trail, Kissimmee, FL 34746
(800) 64-PALMS

Kissimmee and St. Cloud, on the south side of Orlando, in the shadow of Walt Disney World, were once the center of Florida's cattle country. Surprisingly, although they've become bedroom communities for the great magical resort, they have managed to retain their cowboy identity. Kissimmee hosts some of the nation's best-known rodeos. The campground at Tropical Palms is, by any standards, a large one, but it doesn't give that impression. The sites are large, spacious, and grassy. Some are shaded, some open, and all are separated by trees that give the resort an enclosed, intimate, atmosphere.

FACILITIES: Of the 540 sites, 450 have full-service hookups to 30 amps, cable TV and telephone, and 400 are pull-throughs. Forty more have water and electric hookups, and 50 have none. There are also 120 one- and two-room vacation cottages, all self-contained, and all with fully-equipped kitchens. The bathhouses are clean and well-managed, and the laundry room is equipped with the best commercial machines. Sewage disposal is available for overnight campers.

RULES & REGULATIONS: Pets are welcome but must be kept under control. Tenters are welcome, too. The quiet time is 10 PM to 7 AM.

SECURITY: Excellent. Traffic control and on-site security staff 24-hours.

NEAREST SERVICES: There's a full-service store on the property where you can buy groceries, paper goods, gifts, and camping supplies. There's also an outdoor café where you can get snacks and a light meal. Better yet, there are more than 70 shops, restaurants, and attractions within walking distance of the resort.

RECREATION: There's a large, well-equipped recreation hall and activity center, and a heated swimming pool with plenty of furniture and lots of room to relax in the sunshine. There's a playground for the kids, two tennis courts, and all the usual court games. Free shuttle service is available for a ride into town. A resident recreation director is on hand to look after your needs, answer your questions, organize tours, and provide a program of planned group activities during the winter months. If you like to fish, Lakes Tohopekaliga and East Tohopekaliga are both less than six miles away, have public access boat ramps, and are well-stocked with largemouth bass, crappie, shellcracker, and channel catfish. If you like to play golf, you'll find the Airport Inn Golf Club south of Kissimmee and the Buenaventura Lakes West Country Club just to the east city.

NEARBY ATTRACTIONS: Walt Disney World is only minutes away and Sea World is even closer off Interstate 75. Orlando is less than 15 miles to the north via Interstate 4. The east coast is 35 miles away via Highways 417 and 528, and the west coast (Tampa/St.Pete) are less than an hour, also via Interstate 4. In Kissimmee, you might like to visit Water Mania, a 38-acre park with a wave pool and 14 waterslides and flumes (6073 W Irlo Bronson Memorial Highway; 9:30AM-8PM during summer; 11AM-5PM winter; $15; 800-527-3092). Splendid China (3000 Splendid China Blvd.; $15; 800-244-6226), is a Chinese-themed attraction with exhibits that include a half-mile-long replica of the Great Wall (handicapped accessible). Check the other listings in this section for more attractions.

RATES: Campsites start at around $20 per night for two persons. The rate for a one-room studio cottage, depending upon the season, is between $59 and $99 per night. For a two-room cottage the range is $69 to $119.

OPEN: Year round.

HOW TO GET THERE: From Exit 25A on Interstate 4, drive one mile east on Highway 92 and turn right onto Holiday Trail.

Lakeland

Sanlan Ranch Campground

3929 US 98 South, Lakeland, FL 33813
(800) 524-5044

This is one for the golfing enthusiast and the outdoor-lover. Polk County's rolling hills provide a stark contrast to the flat expanses around Orlando. It's an area where more than 600 freshwater lakes provide endless opportunities for fishing and hiking, and the campground is located right on the edge of a magnificent, 18-hole golf course. The campground is a large one, set on more than 800 acres with lots of facilities for camping and recreation. It's claimed to be one of Florida's most scenic private recreation areas. You're likely to see alligators relaxing at the lakeside and more than 90 species of wild birds on the property.

FACILITIES: Of the more than 500 sites, 317 have full-service hookups to 50 amps. 50 of the sites are pull-throughs. There are six well-maintained bathhouses with handicapped accessible restroom facilities, two dump stations, and a modern, well-equipped laundry room. Sewage disposal is available for overnight campers. There's a primitive camping area for groups.

RULES & REGULATIONS: Pets are welcome but must be kept on a leash. Alcohol is permitted in the recreation hall and at individual sites, but not in the adult lounge.

SECURITY: Excellent. Round-the-clock on-site security.

NEAREST SERVICES: There's a shop where you can buy some of what you need at the campground. The shops and grocery stores in Lakeland are less than three miles away.

RECREATION: Lots to see and do here. Three heated swimming pools provide plenty of room for sunbathing and relaxing. Three shaded hiking trails furnish seven miles of pleasant walking. Miles of scenic canoe trails offer hours of relaxation on the water and the lake provides fine fishing. The recreation hall seats up to 200 people for fun and dancing, and there's an adult lounge where you can get away from the kids for a moment . The centerpiece of the complex is the superb 18-hole Bramble Ridge Golf Course, where you can enjoy your sport on a course that's usually quiet and uncrowded. In addition to the course, there's a lighted driving range and a pro shop.

NEARBY ATTRACTIONS: For more fun and nightlife than you could ever possibly handle, you'll want to drive either west to Tampa/St. Petersburg, or northeast to Orlando. Tampa is less than 40 miles away on Interstate 4, and Kissimmee and the Greater Orlando area is less than 60 miles away, also along Interstate 4. Locally, you can visit the Polk Museum of Art on Palmetto Street in Lakeland, the House of Presidents Wax Museum and the Florida Citrus Tower on Highway 27 in Clermont. Also see Cypress Gardens near Winter Haven, a lush botanical garden with more than 800 species of tropical plants, birds and butterflies.

RATES: Sites with full hookups are $19 daily for two persons, or $106.40 by the week (minimum seven days). Other sites range from

$12 to $17, depending upon location and facilities. The rate for pets is 50¢ per day per animal (cat or dog). For each extra person the rate is $2 per day. Golfing fees are $14 per person for 18 holes, which includes half cart; or $9 for nine holes, which also includes half cart. Off-season foursome rates for 18 holes are $48, which includes cart; and from January to March the foursome rate is $56.

OPEN: Year round.

HOW TO GET THERE: From the junction of Interstate 4 and Highway 98, drive south on 98 for eight miles.

Lake Wales

Lake Kissimmee State Park

14248 Camp Mack Road, Lake Wales, FL 33853
(813) 696-1112

Lake Kissimmee State Park is some 40 miles south of Orlando in a fairly remote area on the shores of Lakes Kissimmee, Tiger, and Rosalie. You will find no crowds, only the quiet sounds of the countryside, lots of peace and quiet, and some of the finest fishing in Florida. The campground, though not a large one, is extremely attractive with lots of opportunities for outdoor recreation, and it's not too far from the bustling attractions to the northeast and west.

FACILITIES: There are 60 sites, of which 30 have water and electric hookups. There are two bathhouses, one on each loop, each with restrooms, flush toilets, hot showers, and both are handicapped accessible. There are also facilities for primitive camping and another site set aside for use by non-profit groups for youth camping.

RULES & REGULATIONS: No pets, but guide dogs are welcome. Alcohol and firearms prohibited. Do not feed wild animals.

SECURITY: Very good. Round-the-clock security by a resident park manager. The gates are locked from sunset to 8 AM. Campers are provided with the combination to the gate lock, allowing free exit and access after the park has closed.

NEAREST SERVICES: The nearest services of any kind are 15 miles away in Lake Wales, so be sure to stock up before you arrive.

RECREATION: Lake Kissimmee represents nature and the great outdoors at its best. There's as much to do on the water as there is on the land. The fishing on the lake is claimed to be the best in Florida. For sure, you'll find plenty of largemouth, smallmouth and sunshine bass, crappie, shellcracker, and catfish. Other water-related activities include boating, sailing, canoeing, and water-skiing. There's a public access boat ramp on the property, another provides access to Lake Rosalie, and passage onto Tiger Lake is made by boat from Lake Kissimmee via Tiger Creek.

For nature lovers, the opportunities are endless. Designated by the Park service as one of Florida's best birding areas, it's also home to the white tailed deer, bald eagles, sandhill cranes, turkeys, and bobcats. If you're a wildlife photographer, this is the place for you. Hikers, too, will appreciate the more than 13 miles of trails within the park boundaries. There's also a visitor center with exhibits that interpret the pioneer days of south central Florida (cattle country). A living history demonstration shows what life must have been like for the "cow hunters" in 1876.

RATES: April through October, $8 per night. November through March, $12.

OPEN: Year round.

HOW TO GET THERE: The park is off Highway 60, 15 miles east of Lake Wales.

Frostproof

Camp Inn Resort

3455 North Highway 27, Frostproof, FL 33843
(813) 635-2500

Frostproof is a tiny town of less than 3,000 nestled on a narrow strip of land between Lakes Clinch and Reedy. The resort is a large but quiet campground just north of the city with large o⊦ sites in a semi-wooded area.

FACILITIES: Of the 587 sites, almost all have full-service hook, to at least 30 amps; 193 are pull-throughs. Modern bathhouse⸲ provide all the usual amenities, including hot showers. There's a laundry room, sewage disposal, and a camp store where you can refill your LP gas tanks either by weight or meter.

RULES & REGULATIONS: Tents are allowed. Pets are allowed if kept on a leash. No refunds.

SECURITY: Handled by live-in staff.

NEAREST SERVICES: There are some limited on-site services, but the nearest grocery store is in Frostproof, three miles to the south.

RECREATION: There's a fully-equipped recreation hall where the resort staff provides a program of sheltered entertainment when it rains. Two large pools and a heated whirlpool, provide for swimming and sunbathing. There are eight shuffleboard courts and several other court-type games. The emphasis, however, is on relaxation and quiet country living. Church services are held on Sundays, and the staff provides a program of planned activities in the winter.

NEARBY ATTRACTIONS: Most of the local attractions are north of Frostproof, beginning in the Lake Wales area and expanding all the way to through Walt Disney World into Orlando. Bok Tower Gardens (Burns Avenue, Lake Wales), Chalet Suzanne's Soup Cannery (3800 Chalet Suzanne Dr., Lake Wales) are sites to visit. Lake Kissimmee is a few miles east via Highway 630. The Black Hills Passion Play is performed off Highway 27A near Highland Park. Walt Disney World, EPCOT, and Universal Studios are about 45 miles away via Highway 27 and Interstate 4.

RATES: From $15 for two persons.

OPEN: Year round, but always busy. It's recommended that you make reservations if planning a visit during the winter season.

HOW TO GET THERE: From the junction of Highways 630 and 27, drive north on 27 for three miles.

Orange City

Spring State Park

nch Avenue, Orange City, FL 32763
(904) 775-3663

It was in January of 1766, some three years after England acquired Florida from Spain, that a prominent English botanist named John Bartram explored the St. Johns River and Blue Spring in search of recourses that might be valuable to his government. The campground is in a pine forest within walking distance of the river and spring run. A primitive campsite is at the end of a four-mile hiking trail that winds through shaded hammocks and open flatwoods.

The park is well known as a winter home for the endangered manatee, a large sea cow with big, sad eyes and a gentle disposition. Manatees gather in the warm waters of the spring during the winter months, seeking refuge from the cold waters of the St. Johns River.

FACILITIES: There are 51 sites, all with water and electric hookups and picnic tables, and six family vacation cabins with kitchens and bathrooms. The bathhouse has hot showers, the restrooms have flush toilets, and all facilities are handicapped accessible.

RULES & REGULATIONS: No pets, but guide dogs are welcome. Alcohol and firearms prohibited. Do not feed wild animals.

SECURITY: Very good. Round-the-clock security by a resident park manager. The gates are locked from sunset to 8 AM. Campers are provided with the combination to the gate lock, allowing free exit and access after the park has closed.

NEAREST SERVICES: There's a concession stand on the property where you can purchase a limited range of groceries, snacks, rent a canoe, or buy fishing and camping supplies. There's a Goodings store just two miles down the road.

RECREATION: There's a handicapped accessible boardwalk along the Blue Spring Run. A loop hiking trail winds four miles through the swamps and marshes. Good fishing is available in the St. Johns River and the Lagoon, and there's a ramp and dock on the St. Johns River for boaters and canoeists. Motorboats are not allowed on the Blue Spring Run. Other activities include swimming and snorkeling, nature study, bird watching, photography, and picnicking. The picnic area has tables and grills.

NEARBY ATTRACTIONS: There's always plenty to see and do around the park. The following should give you some ideas. The Bulow Plantation Ruins State Historic Site is three miles west of Flagler Beach, Bulow Creek State Park is on Old Dixie Highway in Ormond Beach, Ormond Beach itself is to the northeast via Interstate 4, and Tomoka State Park is on North Beach Street, also in Ormond Beach. Ravine State Gardens are off Twigg Street in Palatka. Daytona Beach and the International Speedway are to the northeast via Interstate 4. Flagler Beach, where you'll also find the Gamble Rogers Memorial State Recreation Area, is north of Daytona and Ormond Beach. The New Smyrna Sugar Mill Ruins State Historic Site is just to the south of Daytona Beach via Deland and Highway 44. Orlando and Walt Disney World are less than an hour south, and the Canaveral National Seashore and Kennedy Space Center are just to the southeast via Highway 46.

RATES: $14 per night. The rate for the vacation cabins is $50 per night the year round.

OPEN: Year round.

HOW TO GET THERE: The park is in Orange City, two miles west on French Avenue.

Hontoon Island State Park

2390 River Ridge Road, Deland, FL 32720
(904) 736-5309

The island is accessible only by private boat or passenger ferry. Before its purchase by the state of Florida in 1967 it had been a home for the Timucuan Indians, a pioneer homestead, a cattle ranch, and a boatyard. Snails gathered from the shallows of the St. Johns River were the staple food for the Indians, and through the years the discarded shells accumulated to form the two mounds which can still be seen from the nature trail.

The 1,650-acre island, bordered by the St. Johns River and the Huntoon Dead River, is one of Florida's lesser known, though better appointed, state recreational areas. The park is a microcosm of Floridian habitats and wetlands where the wildlife is as varied as the scenery. There are pine flatwoods, palm and oak hammocks, cypress swamps, marshes, river tributaries, even a lagoon. Needless to say, the recreational opportunities are outstanding.

FACILITIES: The campground is not a large one. There are just 24 campsites with water but no electricity. What makes this campground unique are the 48 boat camping slips with full-service hookups. The bathhouse, which services both sites and slips, has hot showers and flush toilets and is handicapped accessible (the restrooms are NOT). There are also six rustic camping cabins (they have electricity but no kitchen or cooking facilities), and a primitive camping site just a quarter mile from the park docks.

RULES & REGULATIONS: No pets, but guide dogs are welcome. Alcohol and firearms prohibited. Do not feed wild animals.

SECURITY: Very good. Round-the-clock security by a resident park manager. The gates are locked from sunset to 8 AM. Campers are provided with the combination to the gate lock, allowing free exit and access after the park has closed.

NEAREST SERVICES: Stores are in Orange City, about three miles.

RECREATION: Activities include canoeing (rentals are available on the property), hiking, nature study and bird watching, picnicking, boating, and fishing; the waters are stocked with largemouth bass, bluegill, speckled perch, warmouth, shellcracker, and channel catfish. You can take a two-hour walk along a hiking trail that begins at the ranger station and follows the Huntoon Dead River to a large Indian mound at the southwest corner of the park. An 80-foot observation tower near the picnic area provides a breathtaking view over most of the island. And, of course, there's a picnic area for all the family to enjoy.

RATES: Campsites are $8 per night. Cabins are $22 for a four-person unit and $27 for a six-person unit per night. The rate at the camping boat slips varies from $11 to $13 depending of the facilities.

OPEN: Year round.

HOW TO GET THERE: The park is six miles west of D
S.R. 44. It can be accessed only by private boat, or by the pa
ferry which operates free of charge from 9 AM until an hour b
sundown. A parking area is provided on the mainland.

Orlando Area

Yogi Bear's Jellystone Park

9200 Turkey Lake Rd.
Orlando, FL 32819

8555 W. Space Coast Highway
Kissimmee, FL 32741
(800) 766 YOGI

No camping guide would be complete without at least one Yogi
Bear's Jellystone Park. There are two in the Kissimmee/Orlando
area, both owned by the same company with little difference between them. Both are large, superbly laid out, and both have an
extensive range of facilities.

FACILITIES: Between the two locations there are more than 1,100
sites, most of them with full-service hookups to 50 amps, cable TV,
telephones, and tables. More than 600 are pull-throughs. There are
12 bathhouses – six at each campground – that are kept in excellent
condition. There are 10 laundry facilities, five at each location,
equipped to provide almost wait-free service. Sewage disposal is
available at both locations.

RULES & REGULATIONS: Do not feed the ducks on Boo Boo's
Pond. Quiet time is observed from 10PM until 7AM. Motorcycles
are not permitted in the park. Alcoholic beverages must be con-
fined to your assigned site. Children under 12 must be accompa-
nied by an adult at the swimming pools. There are no lifeguards on
duty. Pets and tenters are welcome.

SECURITY: Very good. Handled by on-site staff 24 hours.

'S: There are full-service stores at both camp-
n buy most of what you need, and supermar-
away from each. LP gas is available on-site

ion is always a top priority at any Yogi
h campground has a large heated swim-
. plenty of furniture and room for relaxing. Each has
mini-golf course, fun factory, recreation hall, playground, picnic
area, and all the usual court games. Each has a resident recreation
director to answer questions, needs, and provide a full program of
planned group activities during the winter months. The big attractions at Walt Disney World, Sea World, and Orlando are only
minutes away from either campground. The east coast is less than
an hour away along Highways 441 and 528. Tampa/St. Petersburg
and all the attractions on the west coast are less than an hour away
along Interstate 4.

RATES: The rates for two adults per night are, depending upon the
season: tent sites $18; full hookup sites $25 to $31; water and electric
only $23 to $29. $3 for each additional person.

OPEN: Year round.

HOW TO GET THERE: The Kissimmee campground is on Highway 192 just four miles west of the Disney main gate. The one in
Orlando is south of the city. From the junction of the Florida
Turnpike and Interstate 4 (Exit 259), drive southwest on Interstate
4 for three miles to Exit 29. From there go one tenth of a mile west
on Highway 482.

Wekiwa Springs State Park

1800 Wekiwa Circle, Apopka, FL 32712
(407) 884-2009

Wekiwa Springs State Park is an area of wild and scenic beauty that
still resembles the central Florida that once was home to the Timucuan Indians.

Wekiwa Springs is the headwater of the Wekiwa River in an area of
lush, green vegetation – upland hammocks, wetlands, and longleaf pine forests. It's a place where you can observe nature in all its

natural splendor. From the wetland forests that border the creeks, to the dry, sandy pinelands, the area literally teems with plant and animal life.

The Wekiwa River flows eastward for a short distance where it is joined by Rock Springs Run. Together they flow 15 miles to meet the St. Johns River to the northeast. The spring is formed by the rushing waters of underground rivers flowing through limestone caverns beneath Florida's central ridge. Although the park is large, more than 6,900 acres, the campground is quite small, but its location just north of Orlando makes it handy to all the sights and attractions.

FACILITIES: There are 60 sites, all with water, electric hookups, tables, and grills. The restrooms have flush toilets, the bathhouse has hot showers, and all facilities are handicapped accessible. There's a youth campground for use by non-profit groups, a primitive camping area, and a group camp with cabins, a meeting hall, and a central dining facility.

RULES & REGULATIONS: No pets, but guide dogs are welcome. Alcohol and firearms prohibited. Do not feed wild animals.

SECURITY: Very good. Round-the-clock security by a resident park manager. The gates are locked from sunset to 8 AM. Campers are provided with the combination to the gate lock, allowing free exit and access after the park has closed.

NEAREST SERVICES: There's a concessions facility on the property where you can purchase snacks and soft drinks, but the nearest full-service store is a couple of miles away.

RECREATION: Fishing, both in the Wekiwa River and the Rock Springs Run, is excellent: largemouth bass, bluegill, redbreast sunfish, shellcracker, and channel catfish. Canoeing is also a popular pastime (rental canoes are available at the concession stand). The park is also a great place for nature lovers and wildlife photographers. If you're a hiker, or just like to walk, you can enjoy more than a dozen miles of nature and hiking trails; there's even a trail with guide ropes for blind persons. There are also eight miles of day-use horseback riding trails and facilities for trailer parking.

NEARBY ATTRACTIONS: Walt Disney World, EPCOT , and Universal Studios are just a few miles to the southwest (Interstate 4 is 1½ miles from the park). The great lakes, Harris, Eustis, Monroe,

Jessop, and Apopka, are all close at hand with more than 20 public access boat ramps to provide easy access. Lake Griffin State Recreation Area and Rock Springs Run State Reserve are also close by. Dade Battlefield State Historic Site is to the west beyond Lake Harris; the Ben White Raceway is in Orlando, along with the Mead Botanical Gardens. Blazing Pianos is a new rock n'roll bar at the Mercato on International Drive, also in Orlando. The Ocala National Forest is just to the north beyond Lake Eustis. The Early American Museum, Reptile Institute, and Silver Springs Wildwater are all in Silver Springs northeast of Ocala, and Ormond Beach, Daytona Beach, the Canaveral National Seashore and the Kennedy Space Center are less than an hour's drive east.

RATES: $14 per night.

OPEN: Year round.

HOW TO GET THERE: From the junction of Interstate 4 and Highway 434, drive west to Wekiwa Springs Road, turn right and drive on to the park.

Sebring

Highlands Hammock State Park

5931 Hammock Road, Sebring, FL 33872
(941) 386-6094

When Florida's Park Service was created in 1935, Highlands Hammock became one of its first areas of responsibility. Even before that, as far back as 1931, the 4,694-acre area of outstanding natural beauty had been saved from being turned into farm land through the efforts of concerned local citizens. By the time the Park Service took it over it had been open to the public for almost five years. Today, the dreams of the local citizens of the early 1930s have been expanded upon to a point where their park has become, not only a place where people can observe conservation at its best, but a natural refuge for many types of wildlife, including white-tailed deer, alligators, otters, bald eagles, the rare Florida panther, and many species of wild birds. The campground is fairly large, well-managed, exceptionally clean, with lots of opportunities for recreation and relaxation far from the crowds, hustle and bustle of the major resorts, many of which are in fact less than a hour's drive away.

FACILITIES: There are 138 sites with water and electric hookups and picnic tables. The restrooms have flush toilets, the bathhouses hot showers, and all facilities are handicapped accessible. There are also facilities for youth camping.

RULES & REGULATIONS: No pets, but guide dogs are welcome. Alcohol and firearms prohibited. Do not feed wild animals.

SECURITY: Very good. Round-the-clock security by a resident park manager. The gates are locked from sunset to 8 AM. Campers are provided with the combination to the gate lock, allowing free exit and access after the park has closed.

NEAREST SERVICES: There's a small convenience store at a gas station about a mile from the park on Park Road. The nearest supermarket is in Sebring on Highway 27.

RECREATION: There are eight separate nature and hiking trails that wind around the park, and a handicapped accessible boardwalk through the cypress swamp. A paved loop trail through the hammock is available to cyclists (bicycles are not allowed on the nature trails) and bicycles can be rented at the ranger station. There's an interpretive center, handicapped accessible, with exhibits that explain the park's wildlife, plant community, and history. There's also a day-use horseback riding trail available to guests with their own horses (proof of a recent Coggins test is required). A ranger-led tram tour of the park gives visitors a chance to see wildlife in the more remote areas of the park. Rangers also conduct walks and hikes and campfire programs according to season and demand. The picnic area has tables and grills.

RATES: April through November $8 per night. December through March $14.

OPEN: Year round.

HOW TO GET THERE: The park is located on SR 623, four miles west of Sebring.

Walt Disney World

Disney's Fort Wilderness Resort/Camp
PO Box 10000, Lake Buena Vista, FL 32830
(407) WDISNEY

As you might expect, this campground and resort offers an extensive range of facilities and recreational opportunities. The sites are located right inside the WDW Resort, and you'll have access to the Walt Disney World transportation system to the Magic Kingdom, EPCOT, and Universal Studios.

FACILITIES: There are almost 800 sites on 700 acres of landscaped parkland, of which 695 have full-service hookups, including cable TV and telephone, to 50 amps. The restrooms and bathhouses are all handicapped accessible, and so is the transportation system within WDW. As far as the rest of the facilities are concerned, the park has the full-range: sewage disposal, laundry, tables, grills, etc.

RULES & REGULATIONS: No pets. Tenters are welcome.

SECURITY: Excellent. Gated and guarded by WDW security staff.

NEAREST SERVICES: On the property. There's a full-service grocery store where you can buy just about everything you'll need, including RV supplies and LP gas by weight or meter. There are several restaurants nearby, and you can attend non-denominational church services.

RECREATION: Transportation throughout the WDW Resort is free to overnight campers. There's a recreation hall, two heated swimming pools with lots of room for relaxing, a lake where you can swim, boat, or fish (rental canoes, sail, peddle and motor boats are available), you can play golf, tennis, and any number of court games. You can also go horseback riding, hiking, and walking. You can visit the beach and the petting farm, and enjoy Disney films. Walt Disney characters visit the resort.

RATES: Rates start at $35 per night. Call for details.

OPEN: Year round.

HOW TO GET THERE: From the junction of Interstate 4 and Highway 192, drive one mile west on 192, and then north to the park.

Winter Haven

Holiday Travel Park

7400 Cypress Gardens Boulevard, Winter Haven, FL 33884
(941) 324-7400

Set in one of the most scenic areas of Central Florida where the fishing is excellent, the hiking great, and the views from the high ground spectacular, this campground started life as a part of the Holiday Inn organization. Then it became a part of the Best Trav-L-Park Association, only to change hands yet again and come under private ownership. Today, the campground is one of the most popular in the Lakeland/Winter Haven area. It's extremely well laid out; the facilities are extensive, modern, and well-maintained; and the sites are large and attractive.

FACILITIES: Of the 200 available sites, 160 have full-service hook-ups, all are large, most are shaded, and each has a picnic table and 8x20-foot concrete patio. Some sites have concrete pad, and more than 100 are pull-throughs. There are four, well-maintained bathhouses with tiled restrooms and laundry facilities all of which earn the campground consistently high ratings in *Trailer Life*.

RULES & REGULATIONS: Small pets are permited, but they must be kept on a leash and never left unattended. Fires are permitted only in grills. Firearms are not permitted in the park. Mini-bikes and motorcycles may be ridden in the park only when entering and leaving. The speed limit is 5 MPH. The quiet time is 10PM to 7AM.

SECURITY: Good. Provided by on-site staff.

NEAREST SERVICES: There's a grocery store on the property and the city shops, restaurants, and theaters are just 3½ miles away in Winter Haven.

RECREATION: The on-site facilities are extensive and include a large swimming pool, several tennis courts, mini-golf, a large game room, recreation hall, and the usual assortment of court games. Beyond that, there's great fishing on any one of the more than 600 lakes that are scattered all over the area. Hiking, sightseeing, dancing, shopping, and fine dining are accessible. A resident recreation director organizes a full program of planned group activities, and the staff will book your entertainment for you, and provide you with directions to all the interesting sights and attractions. If you want to visit the beach, you need only take Interstate 4 and head either east or west for about 75 miles.

NEARBY ATTRACTIONS: All of the sights, sounds and attractions of the two great metropolitan areas in Central Florida are less than an hour's drive from the campground. The Tampa/St. Petersburg area is less than 40 miles west on Interstate 4, and the Kissimmee/Greater Orlando area is less than 60 miles to the east, also along Interstate 4. Locally, you'll want to visit Cypress Gardens near Winter Haven, a lush botanical garden where you can see more than 800 species of tropical plants, birds, and butterflies. Bok Tower Gardens is in Lake Wales. The Polk Museum of Art is on Palmetto Street in Lakeland; the House of Presidents Wax Museum is on Highway 27 in Clermont; and the Florida Citrus Tower is also on Highway 27 in Clermont.

RATES: Call for rates.

OPEN: Year round.

HOW TO GET THERE: The park is one mile west of Highway 27 on SR 540.

The South

This is the area that comes to mind when most people think of Florida. That's natural, since four of the state's legendary resorts lie within its boundaries.

The Florida Keys are a magical chain of islands that stretch from Miami south into the Gulf of Mexico for more than 100 miles. From Key Largo to Key West, where it's still "anything goes," the islands glitter in the sunshine like a string of pearls.

Florida's south Atlantic coast, from Jupiter through Palm Beach County to Miami, is one long beach after another; one magnificent resort community borders another. Each one is a delight unto itself, and each one has something unique to offer.

Jupiter, Palm Beach, West Palm Beach, Delray and Boca Raton offer, not only some of the finest beaches in Florida, but the best of the performing arts, golf, deep-sea fishing, and spectator sports from tennis to polo. Especially wonderful is the diving; there are literally hundreds of places where you can strap on the tanks and explore the wonders of the ocean.

Just to the south of Palm Beach County, the Greater Fort Lauderdale District stretches from Deerfield Beach, through Pompano and Lauderdale-By-The-Sea, and a host of suburbs that make up an eclectic collection of resort areas, ranging from Hollywood, where a two-mile Broadwalk hugs the beach, to the Wild West town of Davie. Gone are the days when it seemed as if every student from every college and university in the nation descended on the beaches to rampage and intimidate. Today, Fort Lauderdale is one of southern Florida's most popular family vacation spots.

Of course, there's the Everglades, where you can visit, explore, and enjoy the wonders of a vast natural wilderness – more than 750,000 acres of swamps, marshes, and wetlands that make up the most famous wildlife refuge in the world.

Next door, Greater Miami is an international destination for tourists and the jet-set. Ever-changing, ever-growing, this section of southern Florida offers a fascinating mixture of culture, sophistication, and tradition unlike any other. South Miami beach is famous for its art deco, and Greater Miami for its museums, art galleries, theaters, nightlife and restaurants, while the Miami Zoo is recognized as one of the finest in the United States.

Fort Lauderdale

Made famous in the 1960s as the Spring Break capital by the movie *Where the Boys Are*, Fort Lauderdale has come a long way from the rowdy, laid back days depicted by Connie Francis and her crowd. Today, "The Fort" is one of the most popular vacation destinations in Florida; it's also one of the most popular for campers.

The Museum of Discovery and Science in Ft. Lauderdale.

Twin Lakes Travel Park

3055 Burris Road, Fort Lauderdale, FL 33314
(800) 327-8182

This fairly large campground, surrounded by all that Greater Fort Lauderdale has to offer, has an extensive range of facilities, is well laid out and scrupulously maintained.

FACILITIES: This campground lacks for nothing. Of the 374 available sites, all have full-service hookups, and 290 are pull-throughs. All are extra-large, paved, and have picnic tables and grills. Telephone hookups are available, too. The six bathhouses are clean and roomy; the laundry facility is spacious and well-equipped, ensuring you won't have to wait long for a machine.

RULES & REGULATIONS: Pets are welcome provided they are kept on a leash. No tents. The quiet time is 10PM to 7AM.

SECURITY: Excellent. The campground is gated and there's staff on-site 24 hours.

NEAREST SERVICES: Only minutes away in Fort Lauderdale; not an inconvenience.

RECREATION: The opportunities for recreation are as extensive as the facilities. On-site, there's a huge heated swimming pool, a wading pool, a playground, and a large adult recreation room. Court games include everything from shuffleboard to badminton. A resident recreation director organizes planned group activities during the winter months. Church services are available, too. Beyond the perimeter there's swimming, fishing, parasailing, water-skiing, snorkeling, diving, walking, shopping, you name it.

NEARBY ATTRACTIONS: There's more to see and do in the Greater Fort Lauderdale area than could possibly be described here, but you might like to try some of the following: The two-mile-long beachside boardwalk is a neat place to go for a stroll. The Wild West town of Davie has a McDonald's complete with hitching posts. Butterfly World is a unique attraction with three acres of tropical gardens and thousands upon thousands of brilliantly-colored butterflies. Flamingo Gardens and Arboretum offer a 1½ mile tram ride through the citrus groves and rain forest where you can see all sorts of interesting wildlife, including otters, alligators, and birds of prey. You might like to go for a cruise to a tropical island paradise on the *Jungle Queen*, which departs several times daily between 8:30 and 11 PM from the Bahia Mar Yacht Basin in Fort Lauderdale (305-462-5596); the ride will cost around $30 but you'll get your money's worth at the "all-you-can-eat" shrimp and barbecue dinner, and when the boat stops at an alligator wrestling show. Better yet, the Sawgrass Recreation Park offers an exhilarating airboat tour that takes in an 18th-century Indian village and live alligators. You'll find even more attractions in the listing for the Yacht Haven Park & Marina on the next page.

RATES: Call for rates. Reservations are a must during the months November through May.

OPEN: Year round.

HOW TO GET THERE: From Exit 53 on the Florida Turnpike, drive a ½ mile east on Orange, then ½ mile north on Highway 441 to Oaks Road, turn west for .4 miles to Burris and turn north. Follow Burris for a ½ mile to the campground.

Yacht Haven Park & Marina

2323 State Road 84, Fort Lauderdale, FL 33312
(305) 583-2322

This is one of the few waterfront campgrounds in the immediate Fort Lauderdale vicinity, and it too offers all the sights and sounds of the Greater Fort Lauderdale community. The campground is not too large, is well-planned and laid out, offers a lot of extras, and its riverside setting offers direct access to the ocean.

FACILITIES: Of the 250 available sites, all have full-service hookups and patios. There are clean, well-maintained bathhouses and laundry facilities, and sewage disposal is available for overnight campers.

RULES & REGULATIONS: No tents or tent/trailers. Pets are welcome if kept on a leash. The quiet time is 10PM to 7AM.

SECURITY: Good. Handled by on-site staff.

NEAREST SERVICES: There's a supermarket only minutes away, and the shops of Fort Lauderdale are about 10 minutes from the campground.

RECREATION: There's a large, heated, and recently refurbished swimming pool, whirlpool, fully-equipped recreation room, court games, boat ramps into the river, and a full-service marina with boat docks. There's also a recreation director on-site to provide a full program of planned group activities during the winter months. The river provides all sorts of water sports from boating to fishing, as well as direct access to the ocean. Beyond the limits of the campground, Greater Fort Lauderdale, the Everglades, and the Florida Keys lie waiting for you to shop, sightsee, and explore.

NEARBY ATTRACTIONS: Stranahan House (110 SE 6th St.), now a historic museum, was once a trading post for the Seminole Indians. Ski Rixen, of Quiet Waters Park (6601 Powerline Rd., Pompano Beach), offers a unique, boatless approach to water-skiing where people of all ages can try the sport via a cable that reaches speeds from 10 to 45 MPH. Ocean World (17th Street) is the place to go to see dolphins, sea otters, sea lions, and wild ocean birds. You also might like to try a Billie Swamp Safari into the Everglades and Big Cypress Preserve where you'll see all sorts of wildlife, including alligators. The park is located about an hour west of Fort Lauderdale off Interstate 75 in the Big Cypress Indian Reservation. For information and reservations call Lee Tiger & Associates (305) 257-2134.

RATES: Rates start at around $20 per night for two persons.

OPEN: Year round.

HOW TO GET THERE: The campground is at the junction of Interstate 95 and Highway 84.

Hobe Sound

Jonathan Dickinson State Park

16450 S.E. Federal Highway, Hobe Sound, FL 33455
(407) 546-2771

Covering more than 11,000 acres, Jonathan Dickinson is one of the largest parks in south Florida. It's a vast natural area with a great many distinct plant and wildlife communities. Almost 20% of the entire park is covered with coastal pine scrub, a biological community so rare it has been designated as "globally imperiled" by the state.

The Loxahatchee River, now one of the nation's "Wild and Scenic Rivers," winds its way through the park beneath a green canopy of lush vegetation, offering a unique and truly natural world. The park's dunes, coastal hammock, mangroves, and the rich environment of the Loxahatchee riverbank, provide rare opportunities to observe many unique and endangered animal species: gopher tortoise, bald eagle, scrub jay, and Florida sandhill crane. The campground is quite large, well-managed, and has an extensive range of facilities, both for camping and recreation.

FACILITIES: There are two main camping areas with 135 sites, all equipped to handle RVs and trailers to a maximum of 35 feet. Rental cabins are available for those less-than-hardy souls who like to do their camping with a roof overhead. All sites have water and electric hookups, picnic tables and grills. The campground, restrooms, and bathhouses all are handicapped accessible. There are also facilities for primitive camping. Sewage disposal is available, and there are public telephones on the property.

RULES & REGULATIONS: No pets, but guide dogs are welcome. Alcohol and firearms prohibited. Do not feed wild animals.

SECURITY: Very good. Round-the-clock security by a resident park manager. The gates are locked from sunset to 8 AM. Campers are provided with the combination to the gate lock, allowing free exit and access after the park has closed.

NEAREST SERVICES: There's a small concession store on the property where you can buy some of what you need: limited groceries, souvenirs, and fishing supplies; the nearest full-service supermarket is just five minutes south.

RECREATION: There are campfire circles, boat ramps, picnic areas, and many miles of nature, hiking and day-use horseback riding trails with facilities for trailer parking. The hiking trails through the endangered scrublands are accessible either from the parking lot at the entrance station, or from Hobe Mountain. There's also an interpretive center where visitors can join one of the ranger-led tours of the park, or a boat ride along the Loxahatchee River on board the Loxahatchee Queen. You can rent canoes and row boats at the concession facility. Activities include salt, lake, and river fishing (on the Loxahatchee), swimming, canoeing, boating, hiking, horseback riding, nature study and bird watching, wildlife photography, bicycling, and picnicking. And, if you like to play golf there are more than 30 courses within 20 miles of the park.

NEARBY ATTRACTIONS: Port St. Lucie is about 20 miles to the north on Highway 91, where you'll also find the St. Lucie Lock and Dam, and the St. Lucie Inlet State Preserve. Lake Okeechobee is to the west, Fort Pierce and Vero Beach are to the north, and West Palm Beach is to the south, where you can visit Lion Country Safari Park on Southern Boulevard. Stuart, the sport fishing capital of southern Florida, is less than 12 miles to the north on Highway 1. Hobe Sound and the beaches are just three miles to the north, also on Highway 1. Jupiter and its famous lighthouse are five miles to south, and Juno Beach is just south of Jupiter. John D. MacArther Beach State Park is 12 miles to the south near North Palm Beach, and the Elliott Museum, a collection of 14 replica 19th-century shops, is in Stuart. The Hobe Sound National Wildlife Refuge, the Blowing Rocks Reserve, and the Fort Pierce Inlet State Recreation Area, are all less than a 20-minute drive from the park.

RATES: May through November the rate is $14 per night. December through April it's $17 per night. For cabins the rate is $50 per day, or $275 per week.

OPEN: Year round.

HOW TO GET THERE: The park is 12 miles south of Stuart on Highway 1.

The Keys

The "Seven-mile Bridge" overseas highway near Marathon.

Big Pine Key Fishing Lodge

PO Box 430513, Big Pine Key, FL 33043-0513
(305) 872-2351

One of the smaller campgrounds listed here, Big Pine Key is on one of the lower keys about 30 miles north of Key West. The key itself, some eight miles long by two miles wide, is second only in size to Key Largo and is known primarily for its herd of "key" deer, a small animal rarely growing larger than two and a half feet tall. Big Pine Key is not like most of the other lesserl-known keys. It has its subdivisions, supermarkets, and shopping centers, and is very much a small urban community along the Overseas Highway. You'll find the campground is well suited to the needs of those who like to get away from it all, but not so far as to become totally isolated. Its unique setting makes it quite special.

FACILITIES: There are only 109 sites with a maximum capacity of 35 feet, of which 70 have full-service hookups. Tenting is available for rent. The bathhouse is clean and there's always plenty of hot water. There's a modern, well-equipped laundry room, and sewage disposal is available for guests only.

RULES & REGULATIONS: No pets.

SECURITY: Good. Handled by on-site staff.

NEAREST SERVICES: On the property, there's a grocery store where you can buy most of what of you need, including paper goods and camping supplies.

RECREATION: The emphasis here is on the clear warm waters of the Gulf of Mexico and, of course, fishing. On-site there's a fully equipped recreation hall, heated swimming pool, boat ramp, an assortment of court games, and the staff puts on a program of planned group activities during the winter months. Beyond that, the fishing is great, so is the boating, and you can swim and snorkel in the ocean.

NEARBY ATTRACTIONS: You can visit the National Key Deer Refuge on Big Pine Key. Other than that there's not much on the island. Key West and Fort Zachary Taylor are just to the south, Bahia Honda State Park is just a few miles to the north, Long Key State Park and Indian Key State Historic Site are farther to the north, and there are any number of tiny islets and keys for you to visit and explore.

RATES: Rates begin at around $23 per night for two persons. Small as it is, the sites are often booked far in advance. Better make your reservations early.

OPEN: Year round.

HOW TO GET THERE: Drive on down the Overseas Highway to Mile Marker 33.

Bahia Honda State Park

Route 1, Box 782, Big Pine Key, FL 33043.
(305) 872-2353

Bahia Honda features extensive sandy beaches and deep waters close enough offshore to provide exceptional swimming and snorkeling opportunities. But, more than that, the benevolent, tropical climate of the keys has created a natural environment found nowhere else in the United States. It's no wonder that the park has an assortment of rare and unusual plants, including the yellow satin-wood, the gumbo limbo, the silver palm, and the gravely endangered small-flowering lily thorn. A specimen of the yellow satinwood and one of the silver palm have been named as national champion trees. All of these wonders can be viewed along the nature trail that follows the shore of a tidal lagoon at the far end of the Sandspur Beach.

Bahia Honda's geological base is the Key Largo limestone produced by a build-up of ancient coral formations similar to those found on living coral reefs to the south. Due to a drop in the sea level thousands of years ago, the reef emerged from the sea, forming islands of which Bahia Honda is the southernmost exposed point. The campground, though small by Florida commercial standards, has extensive facilities, both for camping and recreation.

FACILITIES: There are 74 pads on three modern campsites, all with extensive utilities, including water and electric hookups, and picnic tables and grills. There's a clean, well-equipped laundromat; handicapped accessible restrooms and bathhouses have flush toilets and hot showers. And there are three fully-furnished duplex vacation cabins offering accommodations of up to eight people per unit, linen service, and utensils.

RULES & REGULATIONS: No pets, but guide dogs are welcome. Alcohol and firearms prohibited. Do not feed wild animals.

SECURITY: Very good. Round-the-clock security by a resident park manager. The gates are locked from sunset to 8 AM. Campers are provided with the combination to the gate lock, allowing free exit and access after the park has closed.

NEAREST SERVICES: The park's concession facility offers a limited range of groceries, camping, and fishing supplies. The nearest full-service supermarket is about five miles to the south in Big Pine.

RECREATION: Because of its unique swimming and snorkeling opportunities, the facilities at Bahia Honda are extensive. The beach, one of the nation's top 10, is handicapped accessible via a special ramp. Diving equipment may be rented at the dive shop in the concession building. Other facilities include a campfire circle, freshwater showers on the beach, a marina with overnight docking and two boat launching ramps, and two picnic areas with shaded tables and barbecue grills. Activities include hiking and ranger-guided walks along the park nature trails, swimming and snorkel-

ing, boating, sunbathing, beach fishing, and deep wat
boat fishing for tarpon, sailfish, barracuda, etc.

NEARBY ATTRACTIONS: Indian Key State Historic Site is on the
Overseas Highway at Mile Marker 78.5. It's accessible only by boat,
but if you can arrange a ride, it's well worth the effort. Grassy Key,
at Mile Marker 60, was once the home of Flipper, the movie star,
and is the location of the Dolphin Research Center which is open
for tours. You can also visit the National Key Deer Refuge on Big
Pine Key at the western tip of the island. Key West, Fort Zachary
Taylor, the Key West National Wildlife Refuge, and many more
interesting attractions, including the Key West Aquarium, and
Audubon House.

RATES: The rate for a campsite is $19 per night. For a cabin,
December 15-September 14, the rate is $110 per night. September
15-December 14, $85.

OPEN: Year round.

HOW TO GET THERE: The park is on the Overseas Highway 12
miles south of Marathon.

Boyd's Key West Campground

6401 Maloney Avenue, Stock Island, FL 33040-6090.
(305) 294-1465

As everyone knows, Key West is about as far south as you can go
in Florida without getting seriously wet. Boyd's campground is
very close to the end of the camping world in the United States.
And, like most campgrounds on the Keys, it's not very big. What it
lacks in size, however, it more than makes up for in aesthetics. The
ocean-side sites are well laid out and maintained, the ocean, is
pristine and inviting, and Key West is everything you might
imagine it to be.

FACILITIES: Of the 130 available sites, 56 have full-service
hookups, 39 have water and electric only, and 20 are pull-throughs.
Cable and telephone hookups are available but at an extra charge.
Tenting is available for rent, and the bathhouse has flush toilets and
hot showers. Sewage disposal is available for guests only, and there

are laundry facilities, ice machines, picnic tables, and patios. City bus service is available at the campground entrance.

RULES & REGULATIONS: Pets are welcome only if they are small (dogs under 30 pounds). Tents are fine.

SECURITY: Excellent – 24 hours with a guard at the gate.

NEAREST SERVICES: Just a few minutes away in Key West.

RECREATION: There's plenty to on the grounds: a large heated swimming pool, recreation room, fully equipped pavilion, coin-operated games, and all the water sports you can handle from skiing to sailing to windsurfing, and from snorkeling and diving to the best salt water fishing in the world.

NEARBY ATTRACTIONS: Key West is an attraction itself. A tiny tropical city with brightly painted shops and stores and neat little restaurants, it has more attractions to see and enjoy than many tourist centers twice its size. Be sure to visit the Mel Fisher Heritage Society Museum (200 Green St.) where you can see some of the priceless artifacts Mel recovered from the sunken Spanish treasure fleets. The Audubon House and Gardens (205 Whitehead St.) is a lovingly restored old house full of fine 17th- and 18th-century furnishings. Fort Zachary Taylor State Historic Site was an important stronghold for the Union during the Civil War. The Donkey Milk House (613 Eaton St.) was the home of US Marshal "Dynamite" Williams, a hero of the Great Fire, and is now a "truly tropical version of Classic Revival" full of antiques and interesting artifacts. You'll find more of Key West's attractions described in the listing for Lazy Lakes Campground.

RATES: Call for rates.

OPEN: Year round.

HOW TO GET THERE: Turn left at Mile Marker 5 and drive three blocks south on MacDonald Avenue.

Fiesta Key Resort KOA

PO Box 618, Long Key, FL 33001
(305) 664-4922

Fiesta Key, once called Jewfish Key, and Greyhound Key, so-named when the Greyhound Corporation built a depot there, is now the home of one of the finest campgrounds in the KOA system. Surrounded by the warm waters of the Gulf of Mexico, the 28-acre tropical island is a busy, but well-ordered camping city with extensive facilities.

FACILITIES: As campgrounds on the Keys go, this one is comparitively large. Of the 365 sites, 224 have full hookups, 105 water and electric only, and 183 are pull-throughs. Cable TV is available at no extra charge. There's also a tent village and 20 newly remodeled motel units (some with kitchens). The modern bathhouses are handicapped accessible, sewage disposal is available for guests, and there's a fully-equipped laundry room.

SECURITY: Excellent. 24 hour on-site staff and a security gate.

NEAREST SERVICES: On the property. There's a full-service store that carries most of what you might need, but it would probably be as well to stock up with those odd items you can only find in a drug store or supermarket before you arrive. LP gas is available by weight or meter. Gasoline, marine and motor, is available on site. There's also a restaurant and snack bar.

RECREATION: The campground is completely self-contained and can easily fulfill most recreational requirements. Obviously, the ocean provides most of the action, but there's an Olympic-size swimming pool, a game room, recreation hall, whirlpool, and boat ramps for easy access to the sea. The campground has its own marina where you can rent boats, go skiing, fishing, etc. You can swim in the ocean, often from your own campsite, and you can rent bicycles and spend the day cycling along the coast, taking a dip in the ocean whenever you might feel like it.

NEARBY ATTRACTIONS: Key West is about 70 miles south, Miami is quite a distance away to the north. Grassy Key, just to the south at Mile Marker 60, once the home of Flipper, the movie star, is the location of the Dolphin Research Center, which is open for tours. A little farther south you'll find Marathon, where you can visit the Museum of Natural History of the Florida Keys. Other than that, there are a hundred-and-one tiny keys and islets you can visit, if you have a boat, and the Overseas Highway with its great ocean views is an attraction all its own.

RATES: For a tent site you'll pay $31.95 per night for two persons; a site with water and electric only is $49.95. A full-service site is $54.95. There is no extra charge for electricity and air-conditioning.

OPEN: Year round.

HOW TO GET THERE: From Miami, drive south on the Overseas Highway to Mile Marker 70.

John Pennekamp Coral Reef State Park

PO Box 487, Key Largo, FL 33037
(305) 451-1202

John Pennekamp was the first underwater state park in the United States. The park covers some 70 nautical square miles of coral reefs, seagrass beds, and mangrove swamps. The park is an important one, in that it was designated to preserve a portion of the only living coral reef in the continental United States.

Coral reefs are many thousands of years in the making, formed from the skeletal remains of the living corals and other plants and animals, all cemented together by limestone secretions and calcareous algae. The coral reef is an extremely fragile world, easily damaged by the interference of humans, and by chemical pollution which kills the coral. The Florida Park service is determined to see that such a catastrophe never happens at John Pennekamp. The park encompasses some 53,660 acres of submerged land, and about 2,350 acres of uplands. The uplands make up a varied and natural habitat for many rare and endangered plants and marine animals. As vast as the park is, the campground itself is quite small but unique.

FACILITIES: There are 47 sites, of which all have fresh water and electrical hookups, and picnic tables. The restrooms and bathouse are handicapped accessible, there's always plenty of hot water for the showers, and there are a number of public telephones on the property; sewage disposal is available, too.

RULES & REGULATIONS: No pets, but guide dogs are welcome. Alcohol and firearms prohibited. Do not feed wild animals.

SECURITY: Very good. Round-the-clock security by a resident park manager. The gates are locked from sunset to 8 AM. Campers are provided with the combination to the gate lock, allowing free exit and access after the park has closed.

NEAREST SERVICES: There is a concession facility on the property where you can buy snacks and drinks, but you'll need to stock up on groceries and other essentials before you arrive. If you forget, however, you needn't worry, there are plenty of shops and stores just outside the park on the Overseas Highway and in Key Largo.

RECREATION: The Park Service had the handicapped camper very much in mind when they laid out John Pennekamp. handicapped accessible facilities are extensive, and include a boardwalk along the Mangrove Trail, access to the Visitor Center and Museum, and a boardwalk to the beach. There are also boat launching facilities and picnic areas on the property. You can rent canoes, motor boats, and sail boats at the concession facility where you can also take a glass-bottom boat ride out over the reef, a snorkeling tour of the underwater park, or scuba diving lessons. Activities include snorkeling and scuba diving, swimming, sunbathing, picnicking, boating, sailing, windsurfing, nature study and bird watching. The fishing is excellent.

NEARBY ATTRACTIONS: Cape Florida State Recreation Area is east of Coral Gables on Key Biscayne; North Shore State Recreation Area is in Miami east of Collins Avenue, between 79th and 87th Streets; and MetroZoo is at 12400 S.W. 152nd Street in Miami (9:30AM-5:30PM; $5; 305-251-0400). Parrott Jungle & Gardens are at 1100 S.W. 57th Avenue Miami (9:30AM-6PM; $10; 305-666-7834). The Fairchild Tropical Garden is at 10901 Old Cutler Road in Miami (9:30AM-4:30PM; $5; 305-667-1651). The Art Deco National Historical District, also in Miami, stretches from Sixth to 23rd Streets, and is well worth a tour. And, of course, there's a great deal more to see and explore in Miami, as well as the islands to the east, and the keys south all the way to Key West, including Key Largo right next door to the park.

RATES: $19 per night.

OPEN: Year round.

HOW TO GET THERE: The park is located on Highway 1 at Mile Marker 102.5, north of Key Largo. From the junction of Highways 905 and 1, drive south on US 1 for eight miles.

Lazy Lakes Campground

PO Box 440154, Sugarloaf Key, FL 33044-0154
(800) 354-5524

Just 16 miles from Key West, Lazy Lakes is a tropical camping resort on the shores of the ocean where you can fish, swim, and relax. The campground, like most others in the Keys, is a small one with emphasis on peace and quiet.

FACILITIES: Just 100 sites, of which 50 have full-service hookups. The remaning have water and electric only – 14 are pull-throughs. Cable TV is also available. The bathhouse is clean and attractive with plenty of hot water. There is sewage disposal a laundry room. Tents are available for rent, and there are public telephones.

RULES & REGULATIONS: Tents are welcome. Pets are welcome too, if kept on a leash. The quiet time is 10 PM to 7 AM.

SECURITY: Good. Handled by on-site staff.

NEAREST SERVICES: There's a limited grocery store on the property where you can purchase the essentials. The nearest shops are at Key West, 16 miles away, so you might want to stock up before you arrive.

The Hemingway Home at Key West.

RECREATION: The focus here is on the water. You can fish from your campsite, swim, snorkel, kayak, and paddleboat in the ocean or on the lake. There's a heated pool, recreation hall, and a game room. Beyond the camp, you can drive the 16 miles into Key West and enjoy all the sights and sounds of the city, small though it is.

NEARBY ATTRACTI
Key West. You might
where you can see all
from the massive to
and Museum (907 W
writer's six-toed cat
worth seeing and th
S Roosevelt Blvd.)
more local attracti
Campground and

184 The South

all sites have picnic tables. The
capped accessible, and have
disposal is available for ov

RULES & REGULAT
Alcohol and firearm

SECURITY: Ve
park manage
are provide
exit and

NEA
ab

RATES: Call for

OPEN: Year rou

HOW TO GEI ...
Marker 19.8 and turn left on Jo......

Long Key State Recreation Area

PO Box 776, Long Key, FL 33001
(305) 664-4815

Before Long Key was acquired by the Florida Park Service between 1961 and 1973, the tropical climate and the clear waters attracted explorers to the area. It was home first to the Calusa Indians, then to Spanish settlers until, by 1912, with the establishment of the Key West expansion of the Florida East Coast Railroad, the Keys were no longer a remote and inaccessible area for travel. Long Key became an important depot for the railroad and when its owner, Henry Flagler, established Long Key Fishing Club. The Club became a major attraction for some of the world's greatest salt water fishermen. Unfortunately, Long Key's era of prosperity came to a violent end when a hurricane destroyed the railroad depot and the fishing club in 1935.

With the acquisition of the Key and eventual opening of it to the public in 1969, the area took on new life as one of Florida's premier state recreation and natural areas, with a good selection of vacation and recreational opportunities.

FACILITIES: There are 60 sites with a maximum capacity for RVs and trailers to 28 feet, of which 30 have water and electric hookups;

estrooms and bathhouse are handi-
lush toilets and hot showers. Sewage
ernight campers.

ONS: No pets, but guide dogs are welcome.
s prohibited. Do not feed wild animals.

y good. Round-the-clock security by a resident
. The gates are locked from sunset to 8 AM. Campers
d with the combination to the gate lock, allowing free
ccess after the park has closed.

REST SERVICES: The nearest full-service grocery store is
ut 15 miles south in Marathon, but there's a convenience store
Layton on Long Key. It would be wise to stock up with whatever
supplies you might need before you arrive.

RECREATION: The beach, sea, peace and quiet , and the great
outdoors are what this park is all about. If you like to hike, there are
a number of nature trails and an expanse of beach to enjoy. You can
go snorkeling in the clear green waters off the island, or bird
watching off Long Key Point. Canoeing, windsurfing, swimming,
and sunbathing are all popular activities on Long Key, and the
fishing is excellent; the waters are claimed to be the most produc-
tive in the entire United States. There are three nature trails, a
campfire circle, and a canoe trail, as well as an observation tower
that offers spectacular views over most of the island. There's also a
beachside picnic area.

RATES: $17 per night.

OPEN: Year round.

HOW TO GET THERE: The recreation area is at Mile Marker 67.5
on the Overseas Highway.

Key Largo Kampground & Marina

101551 Overseas Highway, Key Largo, FL 33037
(800) 526-7688

Key Largo is at the northern end of the Overseas Highway, close to
Miami and the John Pennekamp Coral Reef State Park where you

can snorkel, scuba dive, or explore all the wonders of the only living coral reef in the continental United States from the comfort of a glass-bottom boat. In a time before man arrived on the islands south of the mainland, Key Largo was a string of islets, each one separate from the other. At first, bridges were built to connect them together. Then, when the railroads came, the channels were filled and Key Largo became a single unit, one long key that stretches all the way to Tavernier with a four-lane highway right down its center. Before Humphrey Bogart and Lauren Bacall made it famous, the island was called Rock Harbor, but enterprising businessmen, seeking to cash in on the publicity generated by the dynamic duo, decided to change it; in 1952, Rock Harbor became Key Largo. The campground is an aesthetically pleasing resort. There are two beaches and the ocean to the east; Miami is to the north; there's more ocean beyond the highway to the west; and the rest of the keys are to the south. It's a large, campground of more than 40 acres, always bustling with people, most of whom are stopping on their way south. Busy as it is, there's plenty of room and you won't find yourself crowded.

FACILITIES: There are 209 sites, of which 171 have full-service hookups, including sewer, cable TV and telephone; 77 are pull-throughs. Tenting is available for rent. There's a well-equipped laundry room, and the bathhouses are kept in good order.

RULES & REGULATIONS: Pets are welcome. Tents are welcome.

SECURITY: Excellent – 24-hours with a gate and a guard.

NEAREST SERVICES: There's a full-service store on the property. There's also a Publix Supermarket and a K-Mart right next door; you'll want for nothing.

RECREATION: The beaches are pristine and well-kept. There's a large freshwater pool, boat ramp, lots of court games, and the staff provides a full program of planned group activities during the winter months. You can rent a bike, go ocean fishing, swimming, windsurfing, sunbathing, and water-skiing. Beyond the campground, the shops are just a short walk away. Miami is a few miles north, and you'll certainly want to visit John Pennekamp which is right next door.

NEARBY ATTRACTIONS: John Pennekamp Coral Reef State Park, the only living coral reef in the continental United States, is a must. If you don't swim or snorkel, you'll want to check it out by glass-bottom boat. You should also try to visit the Theater of the Sea at Mile Marker 84.5, Islamorada, (305) 664-2431.

RATES: Call for rates. Reservations recommended for the months November through March.

OPEN: Year round.

HOW TO GET THERE: The campground is north at Mile Marker 101.5. From there it's ¼ mile east.

Sugarloaf Key Resort KOA

Mile Marker 20, PO Box 469, Summerland Key, FL 33042
(305) 745-3549

This tiny key just to the north of Key West is a little corner of paradise, but busy enough to dispel any feelings of isolation. The resort is one of the larger ones on the Keys. It's well laid out with large, shady, landscaped campsites, many of them on the beach.

FACILITIES: Of the 246 available sites, 160 have full-service hook-ups, including cable TV, and 50 have water and electric only. Tenting is available for rent. There are group sites for tents. The bathhouses are modern and very clean. The laundry room is modern and well-equipped, and sewage disposal is available for overnight campers.

RULES & REGULATIONS: Pets are welcome. Tents are welcome. The quiet time is 10 PM to 7 AM.

SECURITY: Excellent. Round-the clock with a guard on the gate.

NEAREST SERVICES: There's an on-site grocery store where you'll find almost everything you need, including camping supplies, paper goods, RV supplies, marine and motor gasoline, ice, and LP by weight or meter.

RECREATION: The beaches are wide and clean. There's a large, kidney-shaped, heated swimming pool with a jacuzzi and plenty of room for sunbathing. There's a waterfront grill, pub, game room, and an assortment of court games. You can rent motor boats, peddle boats, canoes, fishing and water-skiing equipment; the fishing is excellent. Planned group activities are available during the winter months. And, of course, you can go sightseeing along the Overseas Highway into Key West, which is just 16 miles away to the south.

RATES: A tent site for two persons is $32.95 per night. An RV or trailer site for two persons with full-service hookups on the beach, the rate is $42.95 per night. For each additional adult you'll pay an extra $7 per night. There's no extra charge for electricity, but you will pay extra for cable TV.

OPEN: Year round.

HOW TO GET THERE: Drive south from Miami on the Overseas Highway to Mile Marker 20.

Miami

Everglades/Homestead KOA

20675 SW 162nd Avenue, Miami 33187-3698
(305) 233-5300

Obviously, the Everglades National Park is the big attraction here, and you won't find a campground closer to it than this one, at least on the eastern side. Fairly busy most of the time, the campground is neat, well-managed and very attractive; the sites are large and well laid out.

FACILITIES: Of the 315 available sites, 215 have full-service hookups and 241 are pull-throughs. Kamping Kabins are also available. Large, modern bathhouses provide all the usual amenities, including plenty of hot water for the showers. Tents are welcome and tenting is available for rent. There's a laundry room, and sewage disposal facilities are available for overnight campers.

RULES & REGULATIONS: Pets allowed if kept on a leash.

SECURITY: Excellent, with round-the-clock surveillance, especially at night.

NEAREST SERVICES: There's a full-service store on the property where you can buy most of the basics, including groceries, books, post cards, camping supplies, ice, and LP gas my weight or meter. There's also a snack bar. The supermarkets and stores are just down the road in Miami or Homestead.

RECREATION: The campground is close to the gateway into the Everglades National Park. On the property there's a fully equipped recreation hall, pavilion, a huge heated swimming pool, hot tub, playground, and the usual selection of court games. You can also rent bicycles. Planned group activities are during the winter months, and there are a number of local tour operators to show you the sights and sounds of Miami, as well as the Everglades.

NEARBY ATTRACTIONS: Don't miss the Homestead Historic District with its stores and gift shops. It's just a couple of miles east of the campground.

RATES: Range from $24 to $95 for a tent site to $34.95 for a full-service site with water, electric and sewer. One-room Kamping Kabins for two persons are $39.95.

OPEN: Year round. Very busy. Reservations recommended.

HOW TO GET THERE: From the junction of Highway 1 and SW 216th Street, drive 4.8 miles west on 216th, then ¼ mile north on 162nd Avenue.

Everglades National Park

PO Box 279, Homestead, FL 33030
(305) 247-6211

The Everglades, a vast tropical wilderness of sawgrass prairie, hammock and mangrove swamp that stretches from Lake Okeechobee to the Keys and Cape Sable, encompass most of the southern tip of Florida from Everglades City to the visitor center at Royal Palm. Most of the water in the Everglades, so essential to its delicate ecosystem, comes from Lake Okeechobee. Since the 1930s, however, with the buildup of southern Florida, the supply has dwindled to desperate levels. Canals, levees, and dikes, land reclamation and drainage have increasingly diverted the water, and vast commercial agricultural enterprises have spread right to the park boundaries. Now the National Park's mission is to save the vast wetlands from further deterioration and preserve it as a wildlife habitat.

The Everglades are a unique blend of tropical and temperate plant and animal life. More than 700 species of plants, and 300 of birds, along with a number of endangered animals – manatees, crocodiles, Florida panthers, etc. – make their homes among the swamps and jungles of what has become known around the world as the "International Biosphere Reserve." There are two campgrounds, both operated by the National Park System: one at Flamingo, the other at Long Pine Key near Homestead.

FACILITIES: At Flamingo there are 295 sites; at Long Pine Key 108. Most have tables and grills. None of the sites have hookups, but the bathhouses do have flush toilets and cold showers, and the facilities are handicapped accessible. Sewage disposal is available at both campgrounds.

RULES & REGULATIONS: Pets are permitted in the campgrounds, but must be kept on a leash. They are also permitted on private boats, but are not allowed on the trails and in the backcountry.

SECURITY: Security is good, maintained by park rangers.

NEAREST SERVICES: There's a convenience store at Flamingo where you can buy some of what you need, including a limited range of groceries. It would be wise to stock up before you arrive. The nearest supermarket to Long Pine Key is in Florida City.

RECREATION: You can join in naturalist-led activities such as nature walks and hikes, attend talks, look at the exhibits in the visitor center, take a daytime or moonlight tram tour, go on a sightseeing boat ride, or spend some time fishing or canoeing. Everglades National Park Boat Tours operates out of Everglades City ($10; 813-695-2591). Wooten's Swamp Boat Rides is 35 miles south of Naples in Ochopee on Highway 41 ($10; 813-695-2781). Miccosuskee Indian Village & Airboat Tours are 30 miles west of Miami on Tamiami Trail ($10; 305-223-8388). Shark Valley Tram Tours are on Highway 41 in East Miami ($10; 305-221-8455).

RATES: $5 to $10 per night.

OPEN: Year round.

HOW TO GET THERE: Long Pine Key - From the junction of Highways 1 and 9336, drive 10 miles southwest on 9336. Take Highway 9336 from the main park entrance at Long Pine Key.

Miami North KOA

14075 Biscayne Boulevard, N. Miami Beach, 33181-1699
(800) KOA-8818

This is a very busy, but attractive campground close to the action, ocean, beaches, fishing piers, cruise ship ports, golf courses, Joe Robbie Stadium, most of the convention centers, and all of the attractions. It's well-laid out, not too big, clean and well-managed with plenty of room.

FACILITIES: There are 207 large sites, all of which have full-service hookups; 102 are pull-throughs. One-room Kamping Kabins are available, but rarely can you just drive in and get one; you'll need to book well in advance. Tenting is available for rent. The bath-houses are modern, clean, and handicapped accessible with lots of hot water. There's a roomy, well-equipped laundry room. Cable TV is available at all sites, and there are sewage disposal facilities available to overnight guests.

RULES & REGULATIONS: Tents are welcome. Pets are allowed if kept on a leash. The quiet time is 10 PM to 7 AM.

SECURITY: Security is good. Handled by on-site staff.

NEAREST SERVICES: There's an on-site grocery store, and a supermarket less than a mile away. LP gas is available on the property by weight or by meter.

RECREATION: There's a large heated swimming pool, Jacuzzi, sauna, game room, recreation hall, and an extensively equipped fitness center. There are several good restaurants nearby and a number of fast-food eateries, too.

NEARBY ATTRACTIONS: There's a lot to see and do in and around Miami, much more if you decide to venture beyond its limits. Some places you might like to try include the Lignum Vitae Botanical Tour at Mile Marker 78.5 on the Overseas Highway at Long Key. The Everglades National Park is just a few miles away

Long Key. The Everglades National Park is just a few miles away to the west. You might also take a tour of the Fairchild Tropical Gardens on Old Cutler Road in Miami. Parrot Jungle & Gardens is at 11000 Southwest 57th Avenue, also in Miami. The Gumbo Limbo Nature Center is in Boca Raton on North Ocean Boulevard. If you're an angler, the Pompano Fishing Pier on A1A north of Pompano will suit your needs. If you like to go cruising, you can head out on the Intracoastal Waterway aboard one of several ships that ply the waters back and forth from Jupiter: *Louie's Lady* (US 1 & A1A; 407-744-5550) and the *Manatee Queen* (1000 US 1 & A1A; 407-744-2191). Rates for both cruises range from $10 to $20. To the south, you can drive down the Overseas Highway and visit the Florida Keys and several state parks, including the John Pennekamp Coral Reef Park, where you can go snorkeling.

RATES: A basic tent site is $25.95 per night for two persons. From there the rates range upward to $35.95 for the largest RV site with full facilities; there's no extra charge for electricity and air-conditioning. The rate for a one-room Kamping Kabin is $36.95 per night for two persons.

OPEN: Year round.

HOW TO GET THERE: From the junction of Interstate 95 and Highway 826, drive three miles east on 826, then 1.3 miles south on US 1 to the campground.

West Palm Beach

Lion Country Safari KOA

PO Box 16066, West Palm Beach, FL 33416
(407) 793-9797

The attraction here is the Lion Country Safari Preserve, a kind of theme park with more than 1,000 wild animals. When they say the campground has "all the creature comforts," they really mean it.

FACILITIES: There are 233 sites, of which 211 have full-service hookups, and 160 are pull-throughs; some of the sites have picnic tables and grills. The bathhouses are clean and roomy. The laundry room is well-equipped, and sewage disposal is available to overnight campers.

RULES & REGULATIONS: Heaters are not allowed. Pets are allowed if kept under tight control.

SECURITY: Good. Handled by on-site staff.

NEAREST SERVICES: There's a full-service store on the property where you can buy most of what you need, including groceries, camping supplies, paper goods, ice, and LP gas by weight or meter. There are a number of supermarkets within easy driving distance of the campground.

RECREATION: There's a recreation hall, a large heated swimming pool with lots of furniture and plenty of room for sunning, court games, and a playground for the kids, but the Lion Country Preserve next door makes this campground one of the most popular in south Florida. Discount tickets are available for campground guests.

RATES: $21 per night for a basic tent site to $24 for a site with full hookups; there's no extra charge for electricity and air-conditioning. Weekly, monthly and full-season rates are available.

OPEN: Year round, but extremely busy. Book well in advance.

HOW TO GET THERE: From the junction of Interstate 95 and Highway 80 (Southern Boulevard), drive 15 miles west on Highway 80.

The Southwest & Lower Gulf Coast

This area is as different from its counterpart to the east as you can get. For the most part, it's a quiet area: a land of outdoor adventure, easy living, long lazy days of sunshine, sand, sparkling emerald-green ocean; neat little towns and cities that fit right into the overall pristine picture of a tropical paradise where the classy little shops, stores, restaurants and cafés invite visitors to stop by and stay for a while. Cities like Fort Myers and Naples, where airboats are more common than Cadillacs, lie nestled on the edge of the great swamp to the east and the ocean to the west. The miles of white sandy beaches and the crystal-clear waters of the Gulf could just as easily be a part of the Abacos, Andros, Bimini, Eleuthera, or the Exumas as they are of southern Florida. Just off-shore to the south, more beaches, and yet more beaches. Beaches that surround the islands: Sanibel, Captiva, Marco, Gasparilla and dozens of other atolls, named and unnamed. To the north, even more sand stretches away like a great white ribbon, bordering the ocean from Naples to Punta Gorda and Port Charlotte. Mother nature is the attraction in this region. Here, far from the great cities to the north and east, you can kick off your sandals, kick up your heels, dance into the wee hours, go to bed early, or climb aboard an airboat and roar off into the Everglades: a wild and beautiful place that time seems to have forgotten.

And, if you're looking for nature at its best, you'll find it even closer than the Everglades. The Corkscrew Swamp Sanctuary in Naples, J.N. "Ding" Darling National Wildlife Refuge on Sanibel Island, and the vast Myakka River State Park just to the east of Sarasota, shelter a wide variety of tropical birds and animals in carefully protected habitats. They are perfect spots for bird watchers and nature photographers. Corkscrew features a two-mile boardwalk through the world's largest ancient bald cypress forest. Myakka River covers more than 28,000 acres of wild and scenic beauty.

Marco Island seems as far away from the maddening crowds as you can get but is, in fact, only minutes away from the action in Naples and Fort Myers. Gasparilla Island is where you'll find Boca Grande, home of the rich and famous. And it's to Marco that anglers flock to hunt the mighty tarpon. Here, the "one that got away" is always bigger and always fought harder.

At the very tip of Florida's southwest coast you'll find the 10,000 islands. Are there really 10,000? Perhaps; why not count them for yourself? It shouldn't take more than a couple of years. They are all waiting for you to explore, and you can simply take your pick: tiny islets and atolls, all wind- and surf-lashed, but as wild and beautiful as the day they were thrown up from the ocean floor.

Everglades City is the western gateway to the Everglades National Park. From here, hundreds of airboats take visitors into the depths of the great wilderness, along with the swamp buggies that provide an alternative, yet just as entertaining, mode of transport into the interior.

So, here on Florida's southwest coast, you can have it all. You can get away and relax, or you can enjoy just about all the nightlife and action you can handle. Add the spectacular sunsets, the pristine beaches, and a deep-green ocean, and you have the makings for a superb vacation.

Naples

Naples is nestled on the Gulf of Mexico close to the Everglades, Fort Myers, Marco Island, Gasparilla Island and the 10,000 Islands. It's no wonder, then, that it's regarded as the center, even the gateway, to the great outdoors. More than 15 miles of pristine white sandy beaches offer unique opportunities for swimming, surfing, fishing and shelling.

Collier Seminole State Park

Route 4, Box 848, Naples, FL 33961
(813) 394-3397

Located on the fringe of the Florida Everglades, the Collier-Seminole State Park offers visitors a rare glimpse of what the region must have looked like before the arrival of the first European explorers. The 6,400-acre park features a vast hinterland of vegetation and wildlife typical of the Everglades.

It was during the early 1940s that Barron Collier, a wealthy entrepreneur and property developer, decided to give something back to the state. He purchased the land, designed the park, and, in 1947, turned it over to the state of Florida.

Most of the park is dominated by a dense system of swamplands: mangroves, salt marshes, and cypress swamps, along with pine flatwoods and the rare Florida royal palm. One rather special feature of the park is a tropical hammock of trees characteristic of the Yucatan and the West Indies. As one might imagine, such a lush tropical environment is home to a wide variety of wildlife, including several of the state's threatened and endangered species. The brown pelican calls the park home, as does the wood stork, bald eagle, red-cockaded woodpecker, the American crocodile, Florida black bear, and the mangrove fox-squirrel. Sometimes, with a great deal of patience, it's possible to observe two of Florida's official state species: the rare Florida panther, and the West Indian manatee.

FACILITIES: The facilities are extensive, including 111 sites with water and electric hookups, and 19 tent camping sites. The restrooms and bathhouses have flush toilets and hot showers, and all are handicapped acessible. There's an interpretive center, a 6½-mile hiking trail, an observation platform overlooking the salt marsh, an extensive system of boardwalks, a campfire circle, boat ramp and a dock, picnic area, public rest rooms, plenty of parking, and a concession facility where you can purchase a variety of snacks, drinks, and camping and fishing supplies. Canoe rentals are available, too.

RULES & REGULATIONS: No pets, but guide dogs are welcome. Alcohol and firearms prohibited. Do not feed wild animals.

SECURITY: Very good. Round-the-clock security by a resident park manager. The gates are locked from sunset to 8 AM. Campers are provided with the combination to the gate lock, allowing free exit and access after the park has closed.

NEAREST SERVICES: The nearest full-service grocery store is about eight miles away on Marco Island. Best to stock up on whatever supplies you might need before you arrive.

RECREATION: Fishing, canoeing the Blackwater River and the Ten Thousand Islands of the Gulf of Mexico, hiking the 6½-mile trail through the pine flatwoods and the cypress swamp, walking the nature trail and boardwalk system, nature study and bird watching, wildlife photography, and picnicking.

NEARBY ATTRACTIONS: Marco Island, Cayo Costa State Park, the Myakka River State Park, Sarasota Jungle Gardens, Warm Springs, the National Police Museum at North Port, Gasparilla Island, the Cape Haze Aquatic Preserve, the Boca Grande Lighthouse, the city of Fort Myers, Lover's Key State Recreation Area, the Everglades Wonder Gardens at Bonita Springs, the Sanibel Lighthouse on Sanibel Island, Port Charlotte Beach near Englewood, the Circus Winter Quarters at Venice, the Fakahatchee Strand State Preserve just a few miles to the south of the park, the Thomas Edison Home at Fort Myers, Rookery Bay National Estuarine Sanctuary a few miles to the north near Naples, the "African Safari" at Caribbean Gardens also near Naples, and the Delnor-Wiggins Pass State Recreation Area near Bonita Springs.

HOW TO GET THERE: The park is located some 17 miles south of Naples on US Highway 41.

Crystal Lake RV Resort

160 CR 951 North, Naples, FL 33999
(800) 322-4525

Close to Naples and the Gulf of Mexico, this campground is a true resort. The facilities are modern and extensive, the grounds well laid out and maintained, and all of the attractions, shopping, and recreational opportunities for outdoor vacationing are close at hand. Naples itself claims more golf holes per capita than any other metropolitan area in Florida, and to be the "training grounds for Olympic shoppers." The roads throughout the resort are 24 feet wide with curbs and gutters, and there are sidewalks on both sides. The sites are all oversized, with a minimum of 40 X 80 feet and a 20 X 60-foot concrete pad; there are no back-to-back sites. Special neighborhoods have been constructed for Class A motor-homes only, which feature gardens on both sides of the pad and either back-in or pull-in design (see photo). The sites surround the 54-acre Crystal Lake. Most are on the lakeshore, some on peninsulas; others border a 20-acre nature preserve; all are beautifully landscaped and well-kept.

FACILITIES: There are 293 sites, all with full-service, five-point hookups: water, electric, sewage, telephone, and cable TV. Each site is landscaped with tropical plants and two queen palm trees; each has an automatic sprinkler, picnic table, and yard light. The bath-houses are modern and clean, the laundries extensively equipped, and sewage disposal is available for overnight campers.

RULES & REGULATIONS: Pets must be kept on a leash 6 feet long or shorter and must never be left unattended. Children are welcome. No more than four people per site. No open fires: approved grills only. Swimming is not allowed in the lake. All RVs must be at least 25 feet long and of commercial manufacture. No tents or pop-up trailers.

SECURITY: Excellent. Secured entrance with a guard on duty 24 hours.

NEAREST SERVICES: The Greentree Shopping Center is just minutes away on Immoklee Road.

RECREATION: The recreational facilities here are extensive. You can fish or boat on the lake, or drive into Naples and fish from the famous pier. There's a heated swimming pool with a large patio, lots of furniture, three spas and lots of room to relax in the sunshine. A 9,200-square-foot clubhouse has several meeting rooms for guests to use. There are eight lighted shuffleboard courts, two lighted tennis courts, a 27-hole putting green, a fully-equipped exercise room, and a boat dock and ramp. The beaches are just minutes away. There you can walk, swim, fish or just lie in the sun. There are more than 40 golf courses in the Greater Naples area, and the streets of the city are lined with shops, stores, restaurants, and chic boutiques.

NEARBY ATTRACTIONS: You can take advantage of any one of a number of tours offered by local operators: Mike Fuery's Shelling Charters at Tween Waters Marina on Captiva Island will take you to the off-shore barrier islands for a half-day or full-day cruise (813-472-1025, for rates and schedule). A tour with Collier Seminole State Park Boat Tours on US 41, 17 miles east of Naples, will cost about $5 and is real value for money (813-642-8898). Historic Spanish Port at 500 N. Tamiami Trail in Osprey is an environmental, archeological, and historic site where you can tour prehistoric and pioneer dwellings (under $5; 813-966-5214). The Philharmonic Center for the Arts at 5833 Pelican Bay Boulevard in Naples offers a full program of performing arts (call 813-597-1900 for schedules). You might also like to tour The Shell Factory in North Fort Myers, see the world's largest collection of shells and coral, and browse the arcade for jewelry, gifts, glass, and resort wear (2787 N. Tamiami Trail, 813-995-2141).

RATES: Lake sites $40 daily; off-lake sites $35.

OPEN: Year round.

HOW TO GET THERE: From Exit 17 on Interstate 75, drive east to CR 951, then turn right.

Naples/Marco Island KOA

1700 Barefoot Williams Road, Naples, FL 33962
(813) 774-5455

Just six miles north of Marco Island and less than 10 miles from downtown Naples and its beaches, this campground is scenic, tropical, and beautifully landscaped with lots of shady palms and thatched buildings. It's also close to some of the best beaches in southwest Florida, several challenging golf courses, and several nature preserves. True, it's not one of the largest campgrounds in the area, but the facilities both for camping and recreation are extensive.

FACILITIES: There are 176 large, shady, grassy sites, of which 146 have full-service hookups and 75 are pull-throughs. There are 17 one-room Kamping Kabins, all air-conditioned. The bathhouses are roomy, kept scrupulously clean, and there's always plenty of hot water. The laundry room is equipped with modern machines and waiting time is usually minimal. Sewage disposal is available for campground guests.

RULES & REGULATIONS: Pets are welcome but should be kept on a leash. Children are welcome. Tenters are welcome.

SECURITY: Good. Handled by on-site staff.

NEAREST SERVICES: There's an excellent, full-service store on the property where you can buy groceries, camping supplies, paper goods, etc. LP gas is available by weight or meter. The nearest shopping center is six miles away on Marco Island.

RECREATION: There's a large, heated swimming pool with a hot tub and patio, lots of pool furniture, and plenty of room to enjoy the sun. There's a playground for the kids with lots of equipment, a large recreation room, and the usual court games. Planned group activities are handled by an on-site recreation director. There's also a boat ramp that provides access to Rookery Bay and the waters of the Gulf of Mexico just beyond. If you don't have a boat of your own, you can rent one nearby, or you can rent a canoe on the property. The fishing, both on Rookery Bay and in the Gulf, is excellent. Exploring the waterways by boat or canoe is a relaxing adventure, there's lots of golf available, and there are several hiking trails for those who like to walk. If you like canoeing, you might also like to try an overnight camping trip to the islands off the coast. Gulf Coast Kayak Company (4882 NW Pine Island Road in Matlacha; 813-283-1125) offers a number of options for nature watching: alligators, manatees, dolphin, etc.

NEARBY ATTRACTIONS: The beaches are just minutes away from the campground in Naples itself, or on Marco Island, which is just down the road to the south. Everglades National Park is only minutes to the south, Big Cypress National Reserve is to the east,

Collier-Seminole State Park is almost next door, and Corkscrew Swamp Sanctuary is to the northeast. A good way to see the countryside is from a hot-air-balloon: High Adventures will take up to three people at a time to sail above the eastern section of Lee County and enjoy a champaign celebration on return (Bonita Springs; call 813-992-3073). No visit to the Naples area would be complete without a visit to Jungle Larry's Zoological Park at Caribbean Gardens, one of Florida's oldest botanical gardens. Here you can wander acres of lush vegetation and lakes that provide natural habitats for a collection of endangered species of plant and animal life from the four corners of the earth. (Daily 9:30AM-5:30PM; $10; 1590 Goodlette Rd., Naples; 813-262-5409.) You'll find many more attractions listed along with the other campgrounds in the region.

RATES: A basic tent site is $29.95 daily for two adults. A site with full-service hookups is $39.95. For a one-room, air-conditioned Kamping Kabin the rate is $42. $95 per night. Children ages 17 and under are $3 per night. Extra adults are $5 per night. There is no extra charge for air-conditioning.

OPEN: Year round.

HOW TO GET THERE: From Interstate 75, take exit 15 and drive south for eight miles on SR 951, then turn right onto Tower Road and drive on for another mile.

Everglades City

Barron River RV Park

PO Box 116, Everglades City, FL 338929-0116.
(800) 535-4961

If you want to get away from it all, you won't find a better place to do it than Barron River. This is the gateway to the Everglades and the 10,000 Islands. Rarely can you find a place where the countryside remains as it was before the explorers of the 15th and 16th centuries set foot upon it; this is one of those places – remote, wild, scenic, primitive, unspoiled. The small campground reflects the ambiance of the Everglades, river, and islands. The sites are large, none less than 1,800 square feet, well-maintained, and close to the water.

FACILITIES: Of the 67 RV sites, all have full-service hookups and cable TV, and 30 are on the waterfront. There are 14 villas and a number of one-room efficiencies for those who might prefer a roof overhead, and there are cabins with just the basics (no kitchens). There's a well-maintained bathhouse with flush toilets and hot showers, but water is at a premium here, so you will be asked to conserve. There's also a laundry room and a snack bar.

RULES & REGULATIONS: Pets are welcome, but must be kept under control and never left unattended. Tents are permitted, but in designated areas only (not a problem). On-board washers and dryers in RVs are permitted only by prior arrangement with management (water conservancy).

SECURITY: Excellent. All vehicles must show pass posted in windshield. Managed by on-site staff.

NEAREST SERVICES: There's no store at the campground, but gasoline, marine and motor, is available. There are convenience stores nearby and grocery stores in Everglades City where you can get most of what you need, but it might be wise to stock up on those hard-to-get items before you arrive.

RECREATION: This is outdoor country: boating, fishing, sailing, hiking, and the like. There's a boat ramp into the river which gives access to the ocean and the islands, but there's little else except for a couple of court games: shuffleboard, basketball, etc. The lack of a pavilion and recreation hall, however, should not cause a problem; there's plenty to see and do. Guided tours and fishing guides are available, and the cable TV system offers 37 channels.

NEARBY ATTRACTIONS: Just the great outdoorscountry. The Everglades National Park stretches away to the south and east, Big Cypress National Park is just to the northeast, the 10,000 islands are just a short distance away to the west, and the Fakahatchee Strand State Preserve is a short distance to the north.

RATES: RV lots $16 to $27 per night for two persons, depending upon the season and whether or not the location is on the waterfront. Villas range from $37 for an efficiency in May to $90 for a two-room villa in January. Cable TV will cost you $2 extra per night or $10 per week. Boat dockage is $5 per day or $30 per week.

OPEN: Year round.

HOW TO GET THERE: From the junction of Highways 41 and 29, drive south on 29 for three miles.

Fort Myers

Fort Myers/Pine Island KOA

5120 Stringfellow Road, St. James City, FL 33956
(800) 992-7202

Pine Island, just to the west of Fort Myers on the Gulf of Mexico, is a quiet getaway spot where you can get close to nature without leaving civilization too far behind. It's a land of beautiful beaches, clear, emerald waters, and spectacular sunsets. The fishing is great, the boating even better, and the opportunities for sun-worshipping second to none. The campground is not one of the largest in the area, but it is secluded and the location is idyllic.

FACILITIES: The sites have full-service hookups to 50 amps; many are pull-throughs, some have tables. There are also a number of one-room Kamping Kabins available. The bathhouse is clean, modern and well-kept, as is the laundry room. Sewage disposal is available for overnight guests. Cable TV hookups are provided and the service is offered at no extra charge.

RULES & REGULATIONS: Dogs and cats are permitted but must be kept under strict control at all times. Tenters are welcome.

SECURITY: Excellent. Handled by on-site staff.

NEAREST SERVICES: There's a store on the property where you can find most of what you'll need, and a free boat ride is provided to the nearby shops and restaurants.

RECREATION: The island is quiet and provides lots of opportunities for outdoor activities, including swimming in the ocean, beachcombing, shelling, walking, hiking, and relaxing. There's a boat ramp, swimming pool, lots of wildlife, a number of nearby golf courses, and the nightlife of Fort Myers is just a short distance away.

NEARBY ATTRACTIONS: Corkscrew Swamp Wildlife Sanctuary, maintained by the National Audubon Society, has guided tours (Route 6, Naples; $5-$10; 813-657-3771). The J.N. "Ding" Darling National Wildlife Refuge, is a 5,400-acre tract of land set aside for wildlife and named for pioneer conservationist Jay Norwood Darling. A booklet provided for you at the visitor center outlines a self-guided five-mile drive through a mangrove forest swamp where you can view a wide variety of wildlife in its natural habitat. There are also canoe trails and nature walks, daily except Friday. (One Wildlife Drive, Sanibel Island; 9-5; under $5; 813-472-1100). Eden Vineyards Winery and Park is where you can taste the fruits of America's southernmost winery (19850 State Road 80, Alva; 11-4 for tours and tastings; under $5; 813-728-WINE). The Edison Winter Home, (2350 McGregor Blvd, Fort Myers) was built in 1886. The furnishings date from the early 1900s and you can see the great man's lab equipment he used during his experiments in rubber research (daily for tours; 9-4 weekdays; Sun. 12:30-4; under $10; 813-334-3614).

RATES: A basic tent site is $24.95 daily; an RV site with full-service hookups is $31.95; and a one-room Kamping Kabin is $39.95. The rates are for two persons. Children under 17 camp free. The rate for each extra adult is $4.95 per day.

OPEN: Year round.

HOW TO GET THERE: At the junction of Interstate 75 and Highway 41, turn west onto Highway 78 and drive to Pine Island. At Stringfellow Road (Route 767), drive on for about 5½ miles to the campground.

San Carlos RV Park

18701 San Carlos Boulevard, Fort Myers Beach, FL 33931
(941) 466-3133

Close to Fort Myers Beach, among the islands of Estoro Bay, this unique RV resort offers a setting of tropical palms, inlets and islands that seems far from civilization but is, in fact, so close to the action in Fort Myers you can almost walk to the shops.

FACILITIES: There are more than 100 sites, all with full-service hookups, including telephone. The bathhouse is clean and well-maintained. Sewage disposal is available for overnight campers and the laundry facility is roomy and clean. There are also a number of efficiency mobile homes available for rent on a daily, weekly, or monthly basis. Linens are provided, but towels must not be taken to the beach.

RULES & REGULATIONS: Pets are permitted so long as they are kept under control. Tenters are welcome.

SECURITY: Good. Handled by on-site staff.

NEAREST SERVICES: There's no store on the property so you should stock up before you arrive. However, the shops, stores, and restaurants in Fort Myers are only a couple of minutes away.

RECREATION: There's excellent fishing from the resort's docks. You can bring your own boat or rent one and try your luck fishing in the surrounding inlets and waterways. Charter fishing boats leave for deep waters daily from the docks just across the road from the park. You can shell in the waters nearby or just across the water on Sanibel Island. If you want to swim, the Gulf of Mexico is just a mile away via a new bike/walk path that leads from the resort to the beaches; you can also rent a bike if you like. There are nine golf courses within 15 miles of the resort. On-site facilities include a heated swimming pool and spa, waterfront picnic areas, a recreation hall, boat ramps and docks, several court games, and planned group activities are organized by a resident recreation director. Bird and nature watching are also popular activities. It's not unusual to see a manatee or porpoise, and there are hundreds of species of tropical and migratory birds on the islands. If you like to go shelling, windsurfing, and water-skiing. Lee County beaches are ranked among the world's best.

NEARBY ATTRACTIONS: To the north, at Punta Gorda, you can take a 90-minute swamp buggy tour through the Babcock Wilderness and Telegraph Cypress Swamp. It's a neat way to explore the great wetlands, and tours leave every half-hour, January through April. The rest of the year, tours are conducted two to four times daily ($10-$20; 813-489-3911). Cabbage Key, an inn on Pineland just to the north, is built atop an ancient Calusa Indian shell mound. It was constructed by novelist Mary Roberts Rinehart in 1938. Accessible only by boat, Cabbage Key has its own nature trails, and a nice dining room where you can enjoy lunch or dinner (813-283-1384). The Calusa Nature Center and Planetarium (3450 Ortiz Ave, Fort Myers; under $5; 813-275-3435) is the place to go for a tour of Florida's native environment. The rustic boardwalks lead past the Audubon Aviary, and the Planetarium features ever-changing programs and laser light shows. Captiva Island is a place where you will really appreciate the Lee Island Coast, and Captive Cruises of South Seas Plantation offer a number of options that includes breakfast, daytime and sunset cruises to Cabbage Key, Useppa, Boca Grande and Cayo Costa Islands (daily from 9; $10-$20; 813-472-7549). The Children's Science Center features hands-on exhibits of electricity, optical illusions, inventions, steam engines, magnets, holograms, the planets, and lots more. When the weather permits, you can view the skies through a telescope. There's also a gift shop and picnic area. (2915 NE Pine Island Rd., Cape Coral; under $5; 813-997-0012).

RATES: May through November $22 daily; December through April $26 daily. Rates are for two persons. For each extra person allow $2 more per day. Efficiency rentals start at around $325 per week; $75 per day when available.

OPEN: Year round.

HOW TO GET THERE: From Exit 21 on Interstate 75, drive 5.7 miles west on Daniels Road, then 5.7 miles southwest on Summerlin, then two miles south on San Carlos Boulevard.

Upriver Campground Resort

17021 Upriver Drive, North Fort Myers, FL 33917-3899
(800) 848-1652

This campground is in North Fort Myers. It's an RV park with large shady lots, extensive facilities, both for camping and recreation, and it's located on the banks of the Caloosahatchee River. Here you can fish for hours in quiet seclusion. Upriver is its name, and upriver it is.

FACILITIES: Of the 298 available sites, all have full-service hookups and some are on the waterfront. The roads are paved, the bathhouses neat and clean, the laundromat modern and well-maintained, and the restrooms are handicapped accessible. Cable TV hookups provide service for a small extra charge.

RULES & REGULATIONS: Pets are welcome but must be kept on leash. No converted buses. Age restrictions may apply during the winter season. Tents are permitted May through September.

SECURITY: Very good. On-site security.

NEAREST SERVICES: Limited camping supplies and LP gas services are available on-site. The nearest full-service stores are just down the road, only a short distance away.

RECREATION: Fishing, boating, hiking, and the great outdoors are the focus of recreation here at Upriver. There's a boat ramp to the river; salt water and river fishing is available on the spot or just downriver in the Gulf of Mexico. The Caloosahatchee Wildlife Refuge is right next door and is ideal for bird and nature watching. If you like to hike, you can walk the river banks for miles. There's a large swimming pool on the property, the usual array of court games, and the staff provides a full program of planned group activities during the winter season. There's also a non-regulation golf course.

NEARBY ATTRACTIONS: You might like to take a trip to Bonita Springs and visit the Everglades Wonder Gardens: a zoo and botanical gardens that feature a wide variety of Everglade wildlife, including bears, otters, deer, wading birds and birds of prey, the Florida panther, and the endangered Everglades crocodile. You can also watch the rather unusual, and somewhat alarming, alligator feedings (under $10; 813-992-2591). Venture forth on an Everglades National Boat Park Tour. These depart daily from the Chokoloskee Causeway on Route 59 in Everglades City just south of Marco Island. You'll tour the 10,000 Islands and the mangrove swamps, see lots of rare and endangered wildlife, including perhaps the manatee, eagles, osprey, alligators, all in their natural habitat ($10; 813-695-2591). The Ford Winter Home in Fort Myers is adjacent to the Edison Winter Home, and you can buy a combination ticket that will enable you to visit both homes ($10; 2350 McGreggor Blvd.; 813-334-3614).

RATES: Call for rates.

OPEN: Year round.

HOW TO GET THERE: From Exit 26 on Interstate 75, drive 1.8 miles east on Highway 78 (Bayshore Road).